God's Inner – City Address

God's Inner-City Address

Crossing the Boundaries

MARK E. VAN HOUTEN
Foreword by Andrew Greeley

**Ministry
Resources
Library**

Zondervan Publishing House • Grand Rapids, MI

GOD'S INNER-CITY ADDRESS
Copyright © 1988 by Mark Van Houten

Ministry Resources Library is an imprint of Zondervan Publishing House, 1415
Lake Drive S.E., Grand Rapids, Michigan 49506.

Library of Congress Cataloging in Publication Data

Van Houten, Mark E.
   God's inner-city address : crossing the boundaries / Mark E. Van Houten.
      p.   cm.
   ISBN 0-310-52011-8
   1. City churches. I. Title.
BV637.V36   1988
253'.09173'2—dc19   88-15328
                                                              CIP

Edited by Lori J. Walburg and Michael G. Smith
Designed by James E. Ruark

Printed in the United States of America

88   89   90   91   92   93   94 / CH / 10   9   8   7   6   5   4   3   2   1

To my loving wife, Rosa,
who has been a steadfast source
of support and encouragement
from start to finish

Contents

Part Four
AVAILABILITY: The Kingly Role

Part Five
GROWING DEEPER: In Deductive Retrospect

Author's Note

Throughout this book all the names of parishioners and most of the names of places have been changed to respect the confidentiality promised to, assumed, or expected by the people who help me reveal truths about the city. Also, I have chosen in places to put on record the actual speech of my parishioners, even when such speech may be crude or offensive. The purpose for doing this is not to shock or offend, but to give greater understanding of the often misunderstood environment of night ministry in the city.

And I heard a loud voice from the throne saying, "Now the dwelling of God is with men, and he will live with them. They will be his people, and God himself will be with them and be their God. He will wipe every tear from their eyes. There will be no more death or mourning or crying or pain, for the old order of things has passed away."

I did not see a temple in the city, because the Lord God Almighty and the Lamb are its temple. The city does not need the sun or the moon to shine on it, for the glory of God gives it light, and the Lamb is its lamp.

Revelation 21:3−4, 22−23 NIV

Foreword

The lesser achievement of Mark Van Houten in this book is to have presented a handbook for ministry in the inner city. The readers who look for guidance in such ministry will not be disappointed. But if that is all the readers find they will have missed a deeper and richer dimension of the book—its theological reflection on the presence of grace.

To write his handbook Van Houten was forced to ask two critical questions: What does life mean? and Where is grace present? Actually they are the same question. While most of us try to answer the question in its first form, usually without finding completely satisfactory answers, Van Houten asks the question in its second form, concluding that God's grace is everywhere, even in the worst neighborhoods and the most dissolute people. The self-communication of God can and does occur in what seem to be the worst possible circumstances.

Even though no respectable theologian or ordinary Christian would deny that premise, churches in fact often behave as if they have a monopoly on grace. They dispense grace to others because God has given them that right. Religious people in my tradition might take such a position more explicitly, but all traditions tend *de facto* to act as though they are grace dispensers.

We know from the Gospel of John, however, that the Spirit blows whither it will. As Nathan Scott has written, for some realities to be sacraments, all realities must be capable of *being* sacraments—capable of revealing the presence of grace in the world.

If it is difficult to persuade church members that grace can be found in ordinary people, it is much more difficult to persuade them that God's grace is disclosed to us in the people Mark Van Houten encounters in his "night ministry." If God is not present among the night people, then he is not present among us.

The omnipresence of God and his grace is a profoundly disturbing truth, the rejection of which is incompatible with Christianity.

You will never find that stand taken more gracefully than in this book.

Andrew Greeley
Chicago
Feast of the Holy Rosary 1987

Preface

Ferris and Sharon abandoned Jarod, their seven-month-old baby. They must have been awful parents! Can you even imagine abandoning a sweet, innocent, helpless infant? What kind of scum did Jarod have for parents? Partyers, probably, who had to decide between one party night per week with Jarod, or two party nights per week without Jarod. These parents surely epitomize the self-centered "me generation" of the eighties. And poor inner-city people that they are, they were bound to be selfish and irresponsible, if not alcoholic or criminal.

This is what we may think upon first impressions. Actually, however, Ferris and Sharon abandoned their baby only after careful consideration of what they believed to be the only other alternatives. Jarod was abandoned after his parents perfected an elaborate plan so that the right person would come to his aid. Jarod was abandoned within the eyesight of wailing, trembling, and desperate parents. And Jarod was abandoned in the firm belief that he would soon be returned to his parents.

Ferris and Sharon were homeless at the time they gave up Jarod. They hadn't a penny left with which to change his diaper or feed him. They were at their wit's end. They planned for me to find Jarod, calculating that I would turn him over to the state Department of Children and Family Services and that this organization would in turn find the parents, provide them with a service plan that would give them the boost they needed toward self-sufficiency and a stable home and, ultimately, restore their son to them. In fact, matters did work out the way Ferris and Sharon had calculated.

You see, things are not always what they seem to be in the big city. Many analogous stories lie behind other seemingly incomprehensible big-city scenes. Unless the Christian is able to interpret accurately what he or she perceives within the inner city, she will be unable to respond in a helpful, appropriate manner. That is the purpose of the present volume. In it I wish to provide a big-city "tour" for all those Christians who live in an inner city, who work in an inner city, or who even occasionally visit an inner city, in order to equip them to provide an effective Christian witness.

If at this point the reader wishes to have both a less inductive and a more comprehensive synopsis of this volume, she is invited to turn to part 5, "Growing Deeper: In Deductive Retrospect." I encourage those who specialize in inner-city missiology to begin with "Postscript: To Fellow Inner-City Missionaries." In the meantime . . .

May I express a series of institutional and personal gratitudes: to the patrons of the Grand Rapids-based Dégagé coffeehouse and its former director, Jack Kooyman, for providing my first experiences in inner-city ministry; to the congregation of the Roseland Christian Ministries Center on the south side of Chicago for teaching me the importance of the Word experienced; to their pastor and his wife, Rev. Emmett and Emily Harrison, with whom I lived and who provided personal tutelage in my education and adaptation to cross-cultural living and ministry; to their pastor-director, Rev. Tony Van Zanten, an inner-city missionary and mentor *par excellence*; to the Seminary Consortium for Urban Pastoral Education (SCUPE) in Chicago for providing one of, unfortunately, only a few seminary programs especially designed to train ministers for work in urban contexts; to the Reverend Father

DePaul Genshe, veteran missionary to women in prostitution; to the Reverend Father Andrew Greeley for his gracious foreword to this book; and to the Northside Ecumenical Night Ministry: director Rev. Tom Behrens, colleagues Rev. Peter Brick, Paul Henderson, and Rev. Jim Reagan. Together may we continue to work toward the realization of the city of God within the city of man in a church without walls.

Mark E. Van Houten
Northside Ecumenical Night Ministry
Chicago, 1987

Part One

APOLOGIA: A Tool Box of Prerequisites

In addition to turf rights, we need to earn the right to come within the presence of others. One way is the Joan Rivers approach: "Can we tawk?" For strategic reasons, such as being written off as a nerd, the Christian will not generally choose this approach.

In conversation with males in "drag" (female impersonators), I make a conscious effort always to refer to them in the female gender. This is in accordance with their own wishes. As a result, many males in "drag" will often seek conversation with me, leaving the door open for God to work in their lives and hearts through me.

Chapter 1

Exegesis of a Community

Once upon a time, I believe it was 1986, a group of big-city officials hired a research company to determine the extent of homelessness within their city. After a long and careful study this company determined the city to have approximately 26,000 homeless people. These same officials, earnestly wishing to improve the plight of their city's homeless, secured the legislation and fiscal means necessary to build enough warm-up centers to accommodate the entire homeless population. With this job complete there remained but one task. Information concerning the availability of these warm-up centers had to be spread among the homeless people. The city officials chose to relay this information to the homeless through—of all things—television announcements. How many homeless people do you know walking around with televisions?

Once upon a time, I do not know when, there was a very successful church. In their zeal to reach ever-higher plateaus of success, the members of this church refused to be complacent. That is to their credit. Yet they had a tendency to jump on bandwagons, the current one being the development of the largest and most comprehensive youth program ever. In preparation, they spent tens of thousands of dollars on facilities and equipment, from classrooms to a gymnasium, from pencils to weightlifting equipment. With facilities and furnishings in place, there remained but one task— recruitment of youth. However, no matter what means of advertisement they employed, the young people never showed up. At the point of desperation, the church hired a consultant to help them figure out how to bring the young people in. After careful and conscientious study of the matter, the consultant reported his findings: Virtually no young people lived in the church's community. That, to say the least, is to their debit.

Once upon a time, I believe it was 1982, there was a very small and struggling church. Wishing the church to grow, several well-qualified members experimented with some creative, attractive programs. But it was all for nought. Then one day the minister had a brainstorm. He embarked on a community study to find out, in addition to what the Census Bureau was able to report, other characteristics of the community that his church served. His single most helpful discovery was that his church was situated in the midst of a colony of divorced and separated people.

The minister considered how the Gospel could best be presented as good news in this context. He advertised for and preached a series of sermons on "The Unbreakable Marriage." He facilitated church members in beginning programs and groups especially designed to appeal to and meet the needs of the separated and divorced. This church tripled in membership and quadrupled in attendance over the course of two-and-a-half years.

The exegesis of a community can pay big dividends to all ministers and missionaries; penultimately, to the community residents; and ultimately, to God. To exegete literally means "to lead out," to work toward understanding. One usually hears the word in connection with the study of the Scriptures. When a theologian exegetes a portion of Scripture, the goal is to gain the same understanding of that portion of Scripture that the original author intended. What if, for example, that author intended a particular injunction to apply only to those who think, speak, or act similarly to those for whom the injunction was originally written? That probability is reason enough to warrant, indeed, to demand that the theologian delve into historical and contextual criticism of the passage. Again, what if a passage of Scripture was meant to be taken symbolically or metaphorically or analogically? Because of such possibilities, theologians need to delve into literary criticism.

No matter how adept an exegete a theologian is, however, it is all for nought if he does not also understand his contemporary audience well enough to lead them to a correct understanding. I will never forget the incident that originally convinced me of the importance of community exegesis. I was the minister-leader of a program for teenagers known as "Teen Time." The church out of which this program is run is the Roseland Christian Ministries Center (RCMC), located in an all-black community on the south side of Chicago. For our first Teen Time "rap session" I introduced a game designed to help the teens and me get to know and feel comfortable with each other. The game consisted of questions which, before they were asked, various teens promised to answer honestly. In return they were allowed to ask me any question under the same conditions.

For warm-up, my questions were relatively nonthreatening. I asked about favorite teachers, hobbies, and pastimes. As time wore on, my questions became more and more personal and threatening, though not unduly so. Finally I asked one young lady if she had every "made out" in the back seat of a car. Immediately a number of the teens, exhibiting hostility that I could not understand, began asking me very pointed and personal questions about my sex life. I enjoined them to keep this game clean. One of them replied, "Well, you asked Dawn if she ever 'made out' in the back seat of a car!" Since I looked obviously perplexed, someone then explained to me my misunderstanding. In the white community, to "make out" merely means to kiss, hug, and perhaps engage in petting. In the black community, to "make out" means to end up in sexual intercourse.

Some communities are much more homogeneous than others and therefore much more easily exegeted. Inner-city communities are invariably heterogeneous and so much more difficult to exegete. For example, Uptown, the Chicago community in which I presently work, reputedly has an ethnic diversity greater than anywhere else in the world. Yet in my own exegetical studies of different inner-city communities, I have also found both environmental and intercultural commonalities, not only from one community to another, but from one inner city to another as well.

The environmental conditions common to inner-city communities are, unfortunately, their dysfunctional aspects. Within inner-city communities children have no adequate areas in which to play. Teenagers also have no place for recreation and thus often form dangerous street cultures. Parents suffer from insufficient privacy because their children are constantly around. Heat and humidity, rats, roaches, and stench make housing conditions unsanitary. Housing costs take too large a share of the family's income. And inner-city conditions breed a lot of predatory crime, such as murder, assault, robbery, burglary; and vice, such as gambling, prostitution, pornography, drug dealing, and loan sharking.

The residents of inner-city communities share some major intercultural characteristics. Irrespective of culture, they emphasize immediate gratification. "Goldbricking," doing the least you possibly can for the most you can possibly get, is a way of life. Residents focus on day-to-day survival. They rely on physical toughness and personal intimidation, often making them boorish, mouthy, and obscene. Alienated from the institutions of society, they cynically reject the police. Finally, their premature initiation into sexuality without the benefits of birth control often results in pregnancy, dooming many young women to a life of financial struggle and single parenting.

One might raise the question: Really now, that is all very interesting, but is "exegesis" really necessary for effective inner-city ministry? In response to this objection, I will describe some actual occurrences of exegetical follies on the part of some inner-city Christians.

Late one night when I was hanging out on a street corner, watching the world go by, a street minister stopped a young girl almost directly in front of me. She couldn't have been a day older than fifteen. The street minister's agenda with her was to impart some theology—literally, some knowledge about God. He explained God as a loving and gracious father who, no matter the degree of selfishness, disrespect, and treason on the part of his children, stood open-armed and ready to forgive and welcome his children back into his presence. Her brown eyes filling with tears, the young girl looked up at the minister and responded, "For years I was beaten and raped by my father but I didn't give up on him either. Two weeks ago he kicked me out of the house and said he never wants to see my face again."

Another inner-city missionary working in the community of Uptown spent over a year establishing trust and rapport, befriending, and serving a large group of neighborhood kids. Confident that he could continue to work effectively with these youth, and feeling that the potential justified the cost, he rented a building. After hundreds of hours of work in surface rehabilitation and transformation of that building into a gym, he invited his young friends to the grand opening. No one showed up. The missionary had failed to take into consideration gang turf boundaries. These young people would not set foot in this new gym if, or rather, *because,* their lives depended on it.

Chapter 2

Networking and Resources

God called me to inner-city missionary work early in my life. So while obtaining my formal preparation and credentials, I began to observe the work of various established inner-city missionaries and ministries. My first observation is still my most significant. In the city of Grand Rapids, Michigan, I both associated with and observed a group of Christians evangelizing among women in prostitution. As we walked down "prostitute row," tracts in hand, I noticed the women, blocks in advance, fleeing at the sight of either—or perhaps both—the tracts and the evangelists.

As the night wore on I observed this behavior time and time again. The women in prostitution who did allow the evangelists into their presence politely refused the offer of a tract. Those few who were willing to explain their disinterest in the religious literature said they had a whole library of the evangelists' tracts at home. Curious about the evangelists' perspective on this matter, I asked one of them why she thought the women ignored the tracts.

Her reply revealed a severe case of myopia further complicated by tunnel vision. The disinterest in the religious literature on the part of the women in prostitution was, in her mind, simply a matter of apostate blood resulting from the work of the devil himself.

Through the night, with one notable exception, the names of women and the places of contact changed, but the story remained the same. Nearly all the women, though shielding themselves from direct, in-depth examination, very politely carried on conversation with the evangelists. That is truly remarkable in light of the fact that the evangelists not only entered the women's place of business uninvited, but also would not take no for an answer when seeking to speak to them.

The exception was a woman, who, when confronted with a piece of the "Gospel," began screaming at the evangelists. Churning with sadness and anger, she confronted the evangelists with her options: "I have five children, my husband has deserted me, Reagan has cut off my aid, and my children are hungry! What the hell am I supposed to do?" I think an act of God kept the mouths of the evangelists shut. They didn't breathe a word. I feared that they would give the answer they later thought of: "Repent and be baptized."

In this context, "Repent and be baptized" is *not* a Gospel message. A Gospel word is, by definition, good news. Although the evangelists were unaware of it, the good news in this context, for all the women we met that night, was that God has resources sufficient to meet their needs and in his providence God allowed our paths to cross; not only so that we could tell them about some available options, but also to tell them that we care enough to be their friends, to provide transportation, to go with them, be with them, and work with them until the justice that God requires is realized.

Those inner-city Christians who are largely unaware of available governmental social services and ecclesiastical resources are poorly equipped to transplant the good news from the city of God into the city of man. "Suppose a brother or sister is without clothes and daily food. If one of you says to him, 'Go, I wish you well; keep warm and well fed,' but does nothing about his physical needs, what good is it? In the same way, faith by itself, if it is not accompanied by action, is dead" (James 2:15–17).

The study of available resources is an ongoing process most effectively done through the method of networking. Minimally, networking requires a phone call to various service providers. Ideally, networking involves face-to-face contact and an exchange of information regarding targeted clientele, services provided, admission criteria, referral procedures, and the like. To personally know the main players in the service industries is to wield a considerable amount of power on behalf of one's parishioners. Believe me, when a parishioner enters such an establishment flashing your business card, he receives the best of available services.

Chapter 3

No Trespassing

The middle and upper class tend to think that because we live in a "free" country we may come and go as we please and where we will within the public sector. This is an arrogant attitude with no basis in the real world. I know a number of people who, in response to such a suggestion, would very likely reply, "Go ahead, make my day!" We can't go where we want; we need to *earn* the right to go on other people's turf and in their presence.

When I worked for the Roseland Christian Ministries Center, one of the ways in which I attempted to earn the right to work in that community was to live in it. I wanted to show my willingness to subject myself to the same vulnerability as others within the community. Of course, vulnerability to the same degree was impossible. I had access to white and middle-class support systems and safety nets that make such an equality impossible. Yet my move showed good faith that was well-received within the community.

Another way in which I sought to earn the right to work in

Roseland was to use my car as little as possible. Again, although I had the choice, my decision showed a willingness, not just to work *for* the people, but to work *with* them. Even more important, this choice showed a desire, not only to be with the people of Roseland, but to be one of them.

Every Christian is different and every community is different. Each Christian must choose for herself what she believes to be the most meaningful ways in which to earn the right to go on other people's turf and in their presence. She must be certain that she is able to tolerate and remain consistent in her choices. These choices, however, are only means toward a shared ownership of the turf and do not in themselves change the status of the new resident Christian as a trespasser.

For roughly the first five weeks of my stay in Roseland I was confronted with comments such as, "Is you lost, honky?" "Massa, go home!" "Fid'na stiff a white boy." No matter how I tried to look as if I belonged, the fact remained that at that point I still did not. Despite "walking tall" and trying to look confident (not cocky!), my eyes advertised fear and uncertainty.

After those five weeks I was accepted almost automatically. With only one exception, I was never verbally assaulted again. That one exception occurred during the last month of my work and stay in Roseland. As I walked home from church one Sunday, little children on my every side playfully chanted, "Hi, Cookie! Hi, Cookie; stay and play, Cookie." An elderly gentleman was concerned whether I thought any disrespect was intended in the nickname (which is a creative and totally irrelevant name, considering that I'm not a cookie eater). Despite seeing my acceptance of it, two people foolishly inquired as to whether white boy was lost. At this point in my tenure it was obvious that just the reverse was true. Not always practicing what I preach against arrogance, I replied, "No, but you must be or else you would know I live around here."

In addition to turf rights, we need to earn the right to come within the presence of others. One way is the Joan Rivers approach: "Can we tawk?" For strategic reasons, such as being written off as a nerd, the Christian will not generally choose this approach. A more common way is the indirect request: "Hello!" or "'S hap'nin'?" or "How's life?" If the person you are addressing responds, you may consider yourself invited into her presence. But to begin talking about just anything could still represent trespassing. Although invited into the home, so to speak, you have not yet been invited to sit down, let alone tour the house.

I used to volunteer time at the Dégagé coffeehouse, a drop-in center for street people in Grand Rapids. There we had the advantage of turf ownership and thus the right to come within the presence of others. Yet we did not have the right to impinge on the personal (as opposed to the physical) presence of others. One evening I was admiring the skill with which a fellow volunteer acquired permission to come into the personal presence of a patron. Step by step she gained permission to dialogue concerning family, health, and finances and to express her concern. But suddenly, in one fell swoop, she overstepped her bounds.

"There is something I want you to know," she said.

"What's that?" the patron inquired.

"God loves you."

"F--- you. I didn't come here to hear that!"

The volunteer had received permission to express *her* concern, not God's. I wonder what the patron's response would have been if the volunteer had said, "I love you." I wonder if the patron would also have come to understand, through her, that God loves him too. What I do know is that at this point in his life the patron was none too sure of God's love, and the volunteer had done nothing to change that.

Chapter 4

Conflict and Safety

There is no doubt that the streets of the inner city can be dangerous. As an inner-city missionary I have witnessed the brutal beatings of women by pimps, a hammer smashing a skull, gang warfare, a knife piercing a heart, a broken bottle slashing a face, and the driver of a car purposely running someone over. I have twice been the victim of an armed robbery and have often been threatened and spit on.

The knowledge I am able to impart on this topic is limited. The ability to handle conflict and avoid physical danger and engage in self-defense varies according to each Christian's knowledge, experience, strength, and various intangibles such as street wisdom and intuition. Only from experience among blacks can an Anglo learn that, among other things, "Fid'na thrown down" can mean, "I am ready to fight." Only by working with gangs does one learn that "popped a cap" means "took a shot" (with a gun). Only through friendship with a Cuban does one learn that the tattoo on his thumb indicates the crime for which he was incarcerated in his homeland.

What I can do is address some issues in preventative maintenance and tell some stories that might help. Prayer and faith should be at the top of your list of preventative measures. I, for one, still believe in miracles. Just being present in an inner-city neighborhood is often enough for one to sense the hurt, bitterness, and anger that bubbles under the surface, on the verge of eruption. That I can go home night after night without suffering more than some occasional damage to my ego and self-esteem after five or six hours in such a volatile atmosphere is a miracle in itself.

Self-awareness is another important preventative measure in regard to safety on the streets. I am not just referring to awareness of one's own weaknesses and limitations; I am talking about a daily, even hourly, evaluation. The Christian must constantly take inventory of his physical and emotional state of being. Did I get enough sleep the night before? If not, will I be less alert and more vulnerable to surprise, retarded judgment, and thus injury? What about my emotional state? Am I angry, and so more likely to bring covert anger to an unhealthy expression? Each Christian must decide for himself the most helpful areas of analysis and the criteria by which they are to be judged.

*   *   *

When you enter a new area of work for the first time you can do two things for your safety. First, get to know various business people—waiters, bartenders, the local firefighters, whoever is there. Let them know exactly who you are, what you are up to, and become their friend. When the streets get too "hot" to handle, these will be places with friends you can run to. Second, do the same thing with some street people. In the event that adversity is directed toward you, you will not have the time to run, or to run would be dangerous. In such cases having a "big sister" or a "big brother" around in a time of danger can possibly save your life. It has saved mine.

Awareness of street activity can also save your life. Pay special attention to the action, movement, mood, and if possible, the tone of conversation among gangs, drug dealers, pimps, and police. Perhaps you may then get a feel for whether or not fights are brewing, the potential for instant conflict, hidden dangers, unseen weapons, and the like. After I have gained their trust, many parishioners have shown me their weapons. For months I thought Sadie had a bum leg until one day she pulled the whole length of a sword out of her pants. When parishioners show you their weapons you need not fear; on the contrary, you may take it as a sign of trust and friendship.

When you walk the streets, show that you are aware and alert. Most victims are people who look like victims. Look people in the eyes. When your eyes meet those of another, you become flesh and blood and less likely an object of potential personal gain. Never cross an alley close to its entrance, and always look directly into it when passing by it. Look in the window of an establishment before entering. By doing so I have avoided walking into the middle of flying fists or slashing blades on several occasions.

Although many dangers on the streets of the inner city are hidden, some can be anticipated. One such hidden danger has to do with timing. The fourth or fifth week of every month is the most dangerous—the money from welfare checks is exhausted, and people become desperate.

The above measures and precautions are equally valid and helpful for both men and women. Both genders need to heed another precaution, but due to a prevailing double standard in our society, it is of particular importance for the women. Men in our society still tend to treat women as sex objects and property. This attitude can be observed in all classes of men, but it is especially prevalent among men of the lower class. Once I actually overheard a man offer the use of his apartment to a homeless couple in exchange for the use of the homeless man's "old lady." To be safe on inner-city streets, women especially have to watch what they wear and how they walk.

There are two criteria by which women who engage in inner-city street ministry should decide what to wear. The first is the need to be agile and swift of foot. In order to dodge a punch or a falling body or flying objects in a brawl that can spontaneously erupt in your presence at any time, it may become necessary to jump, duck, sidestep, or dance your way out of danger. It is usually best to avoid running away as fast as possible, even though it would appear to you to be the surest way to avoid personal harm. Also, there is always the possibility that you may one day need to defend yourself with a punch or a kick; obviously, dresses or tight clothes or high-heeled shoes are a liability in such situations.

Second, the female inner-city missionary should dress (and walk) in a way that exhibits a professional status and communicates self-confidence and control. Dressing in this manner effectively lets any men you encounter know that you are "on duty" and not out to "play"; and that you are satisfied with yourself apart from them and not looking for the "good time" that a man might figure only he can provide for a woman. Tight or tailored clothes or walking so as to draw attention to your female physical attributes detracts from the desired image. Most important, dressing wisely and modestly reduces the risk of degradation, molestation, and rape and enhances the possibility of being viewed not as an appealing member of the opposite sex but rather as a person representing Christ.

I sincerely hope that these remarks do not come across as condescending. I am concerned for the safety of women in this type of ministry because it is my earnest desire to see more women become involved in it. The records of my nightly work as a street minister to homeless youth give clear evidence of my inability to reach females effectively. The ratio of males to females who will trust me enough to seek or accept my help is five to one. By contrast, the women who do the same kinds of work in the Night Ministry exceed this ratio in reverse. It only makes sense. More than 90 percent of the homeless girls and 100 percent of the women in prostitution in Chicago have been abused by men. Why should they risk abuse from yet another male? For these reasons and others, I believe it is not only possible but most desirable for women to work as Christian witnesses and missionaries in the inner city.

I debated at length whether or not to write this chapter. I wish to encourage Christians to work in North America's inner cities, not to discourage it. For this reason I have saved the most comforting advice for last: Never forget that you have access to the full armor of God. Then, when trouble comes, you will be able to stand your ground or, if worst comes to worst, take to your heels for the sake of peace. Paul himself sums up the best protective measures: "Be alert and always keep praying" (Eph. 6:18).

Chapter 5

Sexual Maturity

Sexual maturity is a highly important prerequisite to an inner-city Christian witness. Tales of Christians caught in scandalous sexual behavior and affairs are on the increase. Our sexuality, a precious gift of God, has become a tortured and twisted tool of the devil. Sexual seduction is ubiquitous, but nowhere is it more common-place than in the inner city.

In reality, most women and men are not seduced; they are ready. In this respect the old adage is perhaps as pertinent here as anywhere else: "Your own house must first be in order" (cf. 1 Tim. 3:5). If your own house is in order, the next best precaution is never to allow yourself to enter a compromising situation.

My first and most important lesson along these lines came from Rev. Tony Van Zanten, pastor-director at the Roseland Christian Ministries Center. An attractive young lady entered Reverend Tony's office one day for counseling. She was braless and wore a tight-fitting, low-cut shirt. Tony gave her the choice of going home and getting a bra or counseling in the presence of the administrative assistant, a female.

On a number of occasions women have asked me to provide marital counseling. Each woman did not want her husband to know she went for counsel. Each woman also explained that, for one reason or another, the only place where she could receive counsel was in her own home when her husband was away at work. I guarantee you, I will never know why.

In addition to having your own house in order and avoiding compromising situations, it is also helpful to understand the human need that sexual promiscuity attempts to satisfy. That need is intimacy. The desire for intimacy is one of the primary human drives. Every human being needs to be able to open up with someone, be themselves, be vulnerable, and then still be accepted and able to reciprocate in the same manner.

Such intimacy involves friendship centered in agapic love. It involves love that seeks to give, add to, assist, encourage, sustain, and build up. This is in contrast to a one-sided love that seeks to get, receive, and possess. Petting and sexual intercourse are often cheap substitutes for intimacy. Being short cuts to intimacy, they are rarely successful. This knowledge puts the Christian in an extremely powerful position—he is equipped to fulfill the parishioners' needs beyond their wildest dreams. For who better than a Christian understands and is able to live and model such intimacy? The Christian has experienced the epitome of such intimacy in his relationship with Jesus Christ.

Chapter 6

Attitude and Demeanor

Attitudes and demeanors are very closely related. In fact, I believe it is impossible to separate them completely. My own definition of demeanor is "the nonverbal expression of an attitude." If a person has an arrogant attitude, that person will tend to behave in an arrogant manner.

I could easily make a list of positive attitudes to cultivate and negative attitudes to avoid, and appropriate and inappropriate ways to carry oneself, that would be applicable to all Christians in any context. But there is much more to it than that, especially in the inner city. All Christians everywhere need an attitude of love. How one expresses that love to a person making a living through prostitution, I think you would agree, requires special consideration.

On my first night out in my present job as a missionary, I met a guy named Harvey who was in his mid-thirties. He was sitting in a three-sided doorway to an abandoned building and drinking a

Colt 45 beverage. I was just strolling by when, noticing my collar, he jumped up and graciously introduced himself and welcomed me into his home. "Yeah, yeah, this is my home," Harvey said. "Everyone in this neighborhood knows this is my home and no one messes with me here. I ain't got no light bills or gas . . . and especially rent. And I like it just fine!"

Harvey then gave me a tour of the house. Pointing to his still unopened beer bottles, Harvey said, "There's my kitchen," and to where he had earlier urinated, "There's my bathroom." Seeing some vomit a couple of feet away, I thought to myself, "Now why did he go and regurgitate in the bedroom?" and I began to laugh inside. I didn't laugh aloud since I was afraid that Harvey, although in a drunken stupor, would be aware enough to take offense.

The next thing I knew, Harvey was yelling obscenities at me and accusing me of making fun of him. To this day I am convinced that there was no way Harvey could have read this on my face. My initial reaction was shock. Somehow he had accurately discerned the content of my heart. Quickly recovering from my shock, I denied I found anything funny about either our conversation or his home. Simultaneously I did change my attitude, and fortunately Harvey sensed this. I could justifiably feel humor in this encounter. But I should have saved it for later. I was laughing inside when, as a Christian, I should have been crying on the outside.

Paternalism is an especially lethal attitude in the inner-city work of the Christian. To help someone indiscriminately, to always provide the answers, to formulate someone else's plan of action, and even to offer knowledge of resources are all ways of telling one's parishioner that you do not believe he has the intelligence or ability to do these things for himself. Instead, the Christian's role in such instances is, first of all, to maintain and boost the parishioner's sense of self-esteem and self-sufficiency by showing confidence in the parishioner's ability to think and do for himself.

When this has been established, the Christian is in a position to *facilitate* the parishioner in broadening horizons, enumerating perspectives, considering alternatives, evaluating results, weighing consequences, and so forth. As a facilitator the Christian not only avoids insulting the parishioner, but also leaves the responsibility and consequences of decisions made and actions taken where they belong—with the parishioner. Best of all, the parishioner acquires valuable skills for similar situations in the future, enabling him to help others.

Once while I was counseling with some homeless youth in a drop-in center, one of the young people, Chip, asked if he could have some of my coffee. The drop-in center was not the Night Ministry's, and I was unsure of the rules in this case. Coffee could very well have been a reinforcement item in the center's behavior modification efforts. I told Chip that he was welcome to some of my coffee if he received permission from his primary counselor. About seven minutes later I had finished my coffee and Chip became angry. He accused me of deliberately failing to talk to his primary counselor about the coffee. I calmly replied, "Securing permission from your primary counselor for anything is your own responsibility." Chip was accustomed to manipulating others into taking responsibility for him. My response stunned him, and for once in his life Chip had no comeback—an indication, I think, of his assimilation of a very important concept for the very first time.

One must be especially aware of paternalistic tendencies when crossing cultures. While taking a year of specialized training in urban ministry at the Seminary Consortium for Urban Pastoral Education (SCUPE), I made the acquaintance of another Caucasian who was ministering in an all-black church. One day I asked him to tell me of his most serious cross-cultural blunder. He told me about being on a church committee with three others. The committee had been given the mandate to study and report on new methods of evangelistic outreach in the neighborhood. He hadn't even earned his right to be in the neighborhood but still took the initiative to write a complete report on the matter for the approval and signature of the other committee members. At first he only heard a gracious rebuff. But his real "urban baptism" occurred when he *overheard* them say: "Who does he think he is, taking things over like that— the great black hope?"

Self-righteousness is another exceedingly offensive attitude for a Christian. To the inner-city Christian it quite often means the immediate end of any further relations with a parishioner. I am often propositioned by people in prostitution. I do not know if I will ever get over the shock I experience each time a man or a woman offers to rent his or her body to me for sexual purposes. I must remember, however, that lust itself is a form of prostitution, and therefore neither am I guiltless in this respect.

To say no to a sexual proposition can mean "No, I'm broke." But it can also mean "No, you are too ugly" or "No, I wouldn't stoop so low." If you think about it for even a minute you will realize you cannot possibly explain in religious terms why you do not want to go to bed with a person in prostitution without giving the impression that you are somehow morally superior. That is self-righteousness. That is sin. And that is counterproductive in missions work. After refusing a proposition on religious grounds, I have never yet been able to engage in successful follow-up.

I have made a conscious choice for a lesser evil, a less counterproductive sin. When propositioned by a person in prostitution I usually answer, "No thank you, not tonight" or "No thank you, I've had enough tonight." One night I bailed Suzanne, a female in prostitution, out of jail. In an effort to express her gratitude, Suzanne asked if I was interested in a "freebie."

I replied, "No thank you; I've had enough tonight."

She said, "Yeah, me too." Then what I said sunk in and she asked, "What do you mean you've had enough tonight; you mean you violate your vows?" (Suzanne thought I was a priest.)

I responded with exaggerated surprise, "Oh, I thought you meant coffee!"

After studying my face for a while Suzanne figured out that I was joking and laughed herself silly. From this incident a wholesome friendship developed between us, and Suzanne has since sought help and accepted Christ as her personal Savior and Lord. To God be the glory.

Chapter 7

Language and Perception

In the preceding chapter, the way in which I referred to people who engage in prostitution probably puzzled you. Why did I go through the hassle of saying "person in prostitution" each time, when to say "a prostitute" would suffice? My choice of words has to do with perception. To label someone "prostitute" is to ignore the fact that this person is also a thinking, feeling human being created in the image of God. One might argue that it does not matter what we name others; what we think of others is the important matter. Nevertheless, I contend that how we speak of others will ultimately bias our opinion of others.

I have no empirical evidence to offer in support of my claim. What I do have is page upon page of nightly logged conversations in which parishioners have begged me not to think of them in stereotypical categories. After hanging out in the "Indian Trail Saloon" about an hour a night, four nights a week, for three months, forty-two-year-old Singing Tree called me aside as I was on my way out of the bar. With genuine concern she inquired, "When you sit here and look around at all of us in this bar, do you think we are all alcoholics or bad people?" My answer was simple, direct, and honest: "Not at all." Her reaction, though comparably simple, was deep in meaning: "Thank you!"

Many other parishioners with whom I have worked over an extended period of time have thanked me for not ministering to them in terms of their occupation, skin color, language, or whatever attributes could possibly have taken precedent in my mind over their being fellow human beings. I am certain that it is my language perception of others that is responsible, more than anything else, for many of my parishioners' expressions of pleasant surprise that I am a minister.

I do a lot of ministry among "drag queens" (people in female impersonation). In conversation with males in "drag," I make a conscious effort always to refer to them in the female gender. This is in accordance with their own wishes. As a result, many males in "drag," while deliberately avoiding other Christians with a more provincial perception of them, will often seek conversation with me, leaving the door open for God to work in their lives and hearts through me.

Language and perception are a two-lane, one-way street. How one speaks of another often biases how one perceives another. It is equally true that one's own *way* of speaking will affect how another perceives him. If I were to use improper grammar, for example, others would tend to think of me as uneducated. Regarding biases, Christians need to be particularly aware of the negative bias Anglo-Americans tend to have toward the language of Afro-Americans. We cannot continue to excuse the difficulties recent immigrants have with the English language while holding the black American accountable. The usual argument is that immigrants have both a dialect and words unique to their language while blacks do not. Yet I can readily cite three words and one phrase that have their etymological origins with the African people: yam, canoe, goobers, and "jump the broom."

Rev. Emmett Harrison, co-pastor at the Roseland Christian

Ministries Center, points out that the way Afro-Americans speak is also resultant of a dialect unique to their native tongue. All one needs to do is take note of pronunciation characteristics that black Americans still have in common with their overseas counterparts. All the African languages are soft with no hard consonants, as we call them in the English language. There are no hard endings in the African languages. Just consider the names of their countries: Kenya, Liberia, Libya, Nigeria, Zimbabwe, and so on. Nor are there verb tenses in the African languages. That is why "I go home yesterday," for example, often does not sound peculiar to an Afro-American.

Christians communicate the Gospel message primarily—if not exclusively—through language. If we are unaware of dysfunctional or unjust perceptions that, because of our own language or the language of others, we have toward others, then language can become the door that Satan uses to close off hearts—hearts where we could have worked toward the advancement of the city of God within the city of man.

Chapter 8

Suspension of Judgment

This chapter is closely related to the previous two. Judgment as an attitude and perception must be faced and extinguished by Christians of the inner city. Here I wish to enumerate the reasons, both biblical and rational, for suspending judgment. By "suspend" I mean "to hang so as to allow for free movement of the parishioner." Once a person is judged, it is all over but the tears. If we do not allow a parishioner some freedom of movement, some freedom to change, we might as well put our clerical collar on the shelf with respect to that person.

In the christology of the New Testament, the emphasis regarding judgment is decidedly on its suspension. As I note in more detail in part 5, although Jesus was the only one with the perfect right, he was seldom judgmental. In the Sermon on the Mount, Jesus commands us, "Do not judge, or you too will be judged" (Matt. 7:1). When the church leaders of Jesus' day brought a woman before him who had been caught in adultery, Jesus said that whoever was without fault could throw the first stone (John 8:7). None of them was able to do so under those conditions except Jesus himself, and he chose to forgive her.

Though Jesus was seldom judgmental, that is not to say that he did not confront people with their sin. He disciplined the woman caught in adultery when he commanded, "Go now and leave your life of sin" (John 8:11). But neither did Jesus always verbally confront people with their sin. Sometimes his presence was in itself enough of a confrontation. This can be true for Christians today as well. Often when I am walking the streets of Uptown and come within the sight of those who know me, alcoholic beverages are quickly disposed of, weapons are concealed, fighting ceases, arguments terminate, drugs are hidden, "hustling" (the street word for prostitution) is postponed, and foul language is suppressed—all without my saying a word.

People know instinctively a certain amount of right from wrong. Obviously most people also have a conscience and a sense of guilt about it. I have seen evangelist after evangelist "hitting people over the head" with the Bible. Those are the people and tracts before which people in prostitution flee. Almost invariably the result is further alienation from God. This is perfectly understandable. If it were me, I too would fall more deeply into a subculture of defiance and deviance. If I were convinced that hell was my manifest destiny, I too would live for the moment.

That I am nonjudgmental among my parishioners does not mean that I affirm a theology that is blind to sin in the world. Neither does it mean that I in any way condone sin. What it does mean is that I believe the inner-city Christian ought to save his breath and actions to communicate something that his parishioners do not know. Our calling is to communicate the Gospel, literally, the good news. The good news is that sinfulness is a prerequisite to church membership. The good news is that the church is not a hotel for saints, but a hospital for sinners. The good news is that God is present with, visible to, and available for all his creation.

Part Two

PRESENCE: The Prophetic Role

Moses was nobility and not one of them. Whether from Jehovah or not, Moses' words would merely slide off the hardened backs of Hebrew slaves until he established his presence with them, suffered what they suffered, and became one of them.

This particular McDonald's shows movies around the clock. For the cost of a small cup of coffee or soft drink, anyone can keep warm and be entertained for a minimum of two hours. Across the street some of the means of grace are securely locked behind heavy, beautiful oak doors. Other means are safely asleep on the top floors of skyscrapers or in the suburbs.

Chapter 9

Establishing Presence

Just by virtue of being in a neighborhood that is crime-ridden and permeated with vice, one's presence as a Christian is automatically suspect. Even the clerical collar means nothing to most people in such a community. I have been accused of being an undercover police officer, drug dealer, pimp, reporter—by some people, anything but a minister.

During a three-month period I saw one young man, going by the name "Crook," day after day. Crook was very nervous in my presence. I interpreted that to mean that he was afraid I would preach at him. Around Crook I worked hard at patience and passive perseverance. I walked by him with a nod or a smile and let him observe me in interaction with others. I hoped and prayed that in time Crook would see that I am nonconfrontational, that I as a rule do not preach at others, and that my primary interest and priority is friendship.

There have been cases in which a year was not sufficient time to gain trust and establish rapport, and to my dismay I seemed to be getting nowhere at all with Crook. One day he showed up on the streets with his six-year-old daughter Chrissy. Considering Chrissy a providential inroad, I began to speak to and play with her. Although Crook watched carefully he did not object. With Crook in mind I told Chrissy such things as how lucky she was to have a dad who spent time with her, took her out, and bought her ice cream. In an attempt to bolster my friendship with Chrissy I gave her a stick of gum. As I left I smiled at Crook.

Six days later I met Chrissy again. She was in the Indian Trail Saloon with her father. I talked at length with her. After a time, Crook went to the washroom. Lest I wear out my welcome, I needed to move along, but before I did I gave Chrissy another stick of gum. To sow some seeds for future conversation, I asked Chrissy whether she had any brothers or sisters who might like some gum. She said she had a brother at home, and I teased her about not chewing his gum as I gave her another piece. Crook was still in the washroom when I left.

The very next day Crook spoke to me for the first time. "I know you're a cop, asshole. My friends told me that while I was in the washroom yesterday you interrogated Chrissy about our family, personal lives, and everything. Then before you left you made a phone call."

I never made a phone call. That is against my own street policy. Nonetheless, I learned two very important things. Crook's friends taught me that if they can, inner-city people will invent excuses and cite evidence to write the Christian off. If they cannot discredit a Christian, then his or her presence will embody a prophecy which will obviously disturb them in their present lifestyle. I also learned that only establishing a prophetic presence will open the door to other prophetic means.

Prophetism can legitimately be said to have begun with Moses, who became a standard of comparison for all subsequent prophets to the Hebrews. Moses provides us with an excellent example of a prophet whose prophecy became efficacious only insofar as he established his presence among those to whom he prophesied.

While still living among the nobility, Moses killed an Egyptian who was beating a Hebrew slave. The next day he broke up a fight between two of his countrymen, and one of them asked Moses if he was going to kill one of them as he did the Egyptian the previous day. Moses was nobility and not one of them. Whether from Jehovah or not, Moses' words would merely slide off the hardened backs of Hebrew slaves until he established his presence with them, suffered what they suffered, and became one of them.

The way in which Moses established his presence among the Hebrews opened the door to verbal proclamation. But his presence itself was also prophecy, declaring the same message I wished to give Crook and his friends. It wasn't a message of condemnation, as they had assumed, but the message of Immanuel, "God with us." In the same way, Moses' presence among the Hebrews embodied a number of prophetic messages, the foremost being that God had not forgotten them. Moses was telling the Hebrew people that Jehovah still cared about them, was with them, was willing to reconcile himself to them, and wanted to work with them once again.

*   *   *

Tanya was fourteen when I first saw her. She would sit for hours at a time on a two-foot-high cement bench with her legs crossed and arms akimbo. Her limbs made frequent and involuntary jerking motions that I heard other people call "CJ's" (cocaine jerks). To support her habit Tanya was prostituting herself.

Our paths crossed day after day. For five weeks she would not make eye contact with me. Because of that I knew that even to say hello at that point might drive her away. Finally Tanya did make eye contact with me. At that point I decided that the very next time our eyes met, I would risk saying hello. When the time came, I smiled, but something intuitive told me to leave it at that. I think it was her body language that said, "Don't detain me now." I had no intentions of taking that big of a step, but that could very well have been Tanya's fear, so I let it go.

The next time our eyes met I did say hello to Tanya. To my delight, she said hello in return and did so in a surprisingly pleasant tone. For about a month our relationship, as judged by the length of our conversations, began to develop. One day, about a month and a half after that first hello, I was involved in some informal street counseling when I inadvertently, and literally, bumped into her. She swung around and said, with enthusiasm that caught me totally off guard, "There you are!" Imagine that! Tanya was not only beginning to accept my presence, but also seeking it!

That she accepted my presence *as a Christian* became clear along with the purpose for which she sought me. She introduced me to a friend who was new to the area and explained to her that I was a "church person" and one who could be trusted for help should the occasion ever arise. The only way I can explain this phenomenon is through prophetic presence.

The first person to be described as a prophet in the Old Testament is Abraham (Gen. 20:7). Many scholars dispute the appropriateness of this label for Abraham, since there is no evidence that he ever prophesied in the traditional, verbal sense. It must be that Abraham prophesied by his action, behavior, and example; that is, Abraham prophesied by his presence. Subsequent biblical references to Abraham, in both Old and New Testaments, *never* address the words of Abraham, but rather his deeds (e.g., Rom. 4:3; James 2:21).

*   *   *

Because of the transitional character of the inner city, the job of establishing a prophetic presence is never finished. But this work goes much more quickly among new members of a community once the Christian is firmly established among the more permanent members. For this to happen, the Christian needs to become in a certain sense one with the community.

When I first began to work in Uptown I would often, at the parishioner's request, explain my presence. Invariably I tried to make it clear that I was a Christian-at-large and not a representative of one particular church location. Sometimes I would even say that the streets were my church. Still, I was often asked at the conclusion of my explanation: "Now what church did you say you preach at on Sundays?"

Given that perspective among parishioners, a Christian's message of prophetic presence is sorely limited. Again, establishing a presence that incorporates a prophetic message takes a great deal of patience, perseverance, and time. The prophet Hosea exemplified such qualities. While he was among his people, Hosea's presence became prophetic when all Israel saw how he dealt with his adulterous wife. Gomer and Hosea acted out Israel's relationship with God. Hosea established himself as a warm humanitarian and as fervently patriotic both as husband and as citizen.

With Hosea's presence established in this manner, the Israelites were ready for yet another message of presence. The way Hosea dealt with his wife after the fact was the embodiment of this prophecy; for the worshiper to respond dutifully in slavish and unquestioning obedience is not enough. In other words, Hosea *showed* that God requires of his followers reciprocal participation at the emotional and spiritual levels.

In many respects I pattern myself after Hosea. I live in the community and put up with what my parishioners must put up with. I have been robbed, as many of them have been robbed. I have been intimidated and shown disrespect. I have been the target of spittle on more than one occasion. By hanging in there with the community despite, unlike most of them, having a choice to get out, my prophetic message *shows* my Uptown parishioners that I have no other church to which I can choose to flee and hide. Under these circumstances my presence is prophetic in that it *shows* them that they are worthy, in and of themselves, not only of my work among them, but of the presence of God himself with them.

I know from experience that this medium of prophecy is effective for two reasons. First, it convinces others of my presence as their minister. For quite some time I had been cultivating a friendship with a woman in prostitution named Rehab. For the longest time it appeared that Rehab could not receive a prophecy through my presence. I was convinced that she did not believe I could be her minister in light of her occupation.

God took over where my skills on his behalf were exhausted. As I entered the street one evening, a man appeared who didn't realize that I was no newcomer to the neighborhood. He began to mock me: "Hey, Father, let's see a miracle! Show me your stuff! You know this community could use a miracle now!" Providentially, and unknown to me at the time, Rehab was in the vicinity. Rehab ran over to us, stepped in between us, and shook a finger at the man who was mocking me. Speaking with authority, Rehab said, "Huh-uh. Don't make fun of *my* minister."

Second, I know that by becoming one with the community, my presence as a medium of prophecy is effective because of those who have told me so. As I was strolling down a street one night, feeling particularly useless as a missionary, a middle-aged man asked to speak to me for a moment. His testimony would have provided encouragement and motivation sufficient for the most discouraged or depressed Christian. "Father," he began, "I've been watching you for weeks now. I know you have got to be frustrated at times. But, ya know, you being here does make a difference. Since you've been hanging around I've reexamined my life, taken inventory, rededicated myself to some old resolutions and to God himself. And trust me, you're having a good effect on some others."

*   *   *

In establishing prophetic presence Jesus remains the example *par excellence*. He made a bigger sacrifice than any other Christian will ever have to make. He clothed his divinity in human flesh. He identified with humans to the full. Jesus lived under the same conditions and with the same restrictions humans have to endure. Jesus suffered what we have to suffer and became in that way, in human terms at least, a more relevant and believable prophet. What aided Jesus most in being an effective Christian was his willingness to be Immanuel, "God with us."

As Christlike missionaries we need to embody Jesus' prophetic message that God is with us. The message of Jesus' prophetic presence was not always clear; many people did not recognize him. Our prophetic message is often much less clear. We need to be innovative and creative in our contact with others, helping them to understand the prophetic message inherent in our presence.

Many unemployed, dispossessed, and bored people congregate around the Liftland Hotel, especially during the summer when there are daily "vigils." Despite hardships the atmosphere is pleasant. They have people to talk to, people to be with, and the warm sun on their backs instead of cold snow and the perpetual fear of freezing to death. The only thing that disturbs them from time to time is the police who ask them to move on and threaten to arrest them for loitering. (There is no law in Chicago against loitering. The police will arrest only a particularly belligerent person and then on suspicion of pandering.)

The presence of the police is extremely disgruntling to the Liftland crowd under these circumstances. The inconvenience is minor. The crowd begins to walk away but as soon as the police leave, they quickly settle back in. What is so disgruntling is the rude and abrupt removal of this congregation of people from their all-too-fleeting state of mesmerized bliss in which they are able to suppress their anger at the world, forget their hardships, and become for a while truly carefree.

While I was with the Liftland group one evening, the police had been around three times already. When they pulled up for the fourth time, feelings of exasperation ran high. "Where do they really expect us to go?" a young woman asked. I asked the group to gather around me in a circle and bow their heads. Everyone responded quickly and without exception. The two officers observed in silence for quite some time. Finally one of them asked, "What's going on here?" Looking up, making certain they saw my collar, I replied, "Oh, hello officers. We're having a prayer meeting. Care to join us?" Naturally they did not and moved on without another word, just as I had hoped.

Not quite sure of the situation, Buffalo, an old American Indian, asked whether I had not just lied to the police.

"That's one way of looking at it," I said. "Another way is to say that I provided a temporary haven for the homeless."

Buffalo's son, Jo Jo, chimed in, "I get it. You did what Jesus did to the Pharisees."

"You can hang around here anytime!" Dino exclaimed.

On Wilson Street there lived a fifteen-year-old with whom I made regular contact. She was another of those who would not speak to me for a long time. She struggled with an addiction, so I told her about my own past struggle with alcohol addiction. I also suggested where she could get help if she was interested.

Still this young lady did not seem interested or even able to trust me. Then one night she was about to be taken to jail for being in violation of curfew. In light of her problems overall, I did not think this would be of any benefit to her. (Even if it led to charges being filed against her parent[s] for neglect, it was unlikely to be of help. Very few neglect cases hold up in court. Family reunification is the state policy priority number one in Illinois. Therefore the definition of what constitutes a family is left extremely vague.)

I approached the officer and asked whether there was a problem. When the officer explained, I said, "But officer, she's with me." I signed for her and she was released. Since then, the door to a fuller understanding of my presence as prophecy has swung wide open for this youth.

*   *   *

On another "turf" I have been trying to "get in" with a gang that goes by the name of Vicelords. They too had a tough shell to penetrate. Once when I just happened to be strolling by, I saw another gang, the Gaylords, verbally harassing the Vicelords. The two were on the verge of warfare, and the Vicelords were outnumbered three to one. I carefully let the Gaylords become aware of my presence until they asked who I was. I told them that I was a minister and also mentioned that I had heard a policeman one block away calling for back-ups for possible gang warfare.

The Gaylords left in a hurry. The Vicelords gathered around

me, asking me about the police. I looked at each of them and smiled deviously. Then a member of the Vicelords wrapped himself around me, hugged me, and jumped up and down yelling, "You s.o.b.! You saved our lives!" This particular group of Vicelords is now primed for prophecy.

On the corner of Broadway and Lawrence one night, I flagged down a police car to get the officers to stop a man who was beating a woman. A female officer jumped out of the car and said she was sorry, but they had received a report of a guy wearing a black shirt and concealing a gun so she was going to have to frisk me. When she finished, I directed them to the scene of the beating.

As Jesus identified with humans by taking on our flesh, I saw in this incident an ideal opportunity to take on the flesh of my parishioners. If they knew I had been frisked, as so many of them were frisked every day, this incident would do a lot to help establish my presence as prophetic. All I had to do was "beef up" the story a bit so that it would capture the short attention span of my parishioners.

I told Dino about it first. He was intrigued, so I continued to tell others the story in the same way: "I was on the corner of Broadway and Lawrence. Nearby a man was beating a woman something awful. I flagged down a police car to get the officers to help out. A lady cop jumped out of the car; you know, that little lady cop who carries that big ol' forty-five. Anyways, she jumps out and starts talkin' 'bout a report of a guy with a black shirt like mine that was in the area with a gun. So she says she has to frisk me and I said, "Uh-huh, knock yourself out.'" That story spread bigger and faster than an arrest or a suicide. Soon everyone had witnessed the whole incident firsthand. Most important, the story spread that *our* preacher-boy was hassled by the cops.

My favorite hangouts in the inner city are the gamerooms. For one, I enjoy playing Donkey Kong, Pac Man, and Galaga. But gamerooms are also good places for Christians to linger because where one hangs out involves a prophetic message (see chap. 10). There is a preponderance of blacks in and around a certain gameroom on Wilson Street. For the longest time I tried to establish my presence among this black population in a passive manner. My thinking was: (1) with an aggressive approach, this "honky" is likely to scare them away, and (2) if I just hang around long enough, some of them are bound to be curious enough to make inquiry.

Weeks turned into months and months into no meaningful presence as a prophet, let alone as a friend. As I was hanging out around this gameroom yet one more day, I began to reflect on my ministry experience in the all-black, southside community of Roseland. After only a short time of reflection, I told myself: "Wake up honky! They ain't no way no black folks is gonna be startin' up talkin' with you. In this situation youse gotta infiltrate—let 'em know you an inside-out Oreo, a soul brudda oda udda colo [a soul brother of the other color]."

Conjuring up the accent, dialect, idioms, phrases, and word meanings unique to Afro-Americans, I went to work. I approached a gathering of seventeen black young people and, knowing they were bragging and bantering in fun, I yelled, "Ya'all talkin' yang . . . alla ya'all . . . that's right, s-sma-a-ack! What you-all starin' at? Ain't you never seen a brother from the south [side of Chicago]? That's right. I can jive [banter] wich ya'all. Nah!" (What do you think of that?) The young people were immediately and obviously intrigued and very soon did feel that I was one of them. Some of my most fruitful work as a Christian has been done, and continues to be done, among members of this group.

*   *   *

To be a Christian is in itself nothing. To be a Christian who verbalizes the gospel message is at times necessary, appropriate to the circumstances, and the only way to prophesy. In other contexts verbal prophecy may not be conducive to the circumstances for initiating discipleship. In such cases let Jesus be your example. At least initially, allow your presence to be prophetic. Jesus showed that, in addition to *how* one establishes presence, even *where* one establishes presence is prophetic. That is the subject of chapter 10.

Places of Presence

Once upon a time there was a Christian in the inner city who was a seasoned orator and beyond compare in her ability to win souls for Christ through verbal proclamation of the Gospel. Eloquence alone was enough to win scores of people. Her imagination and verbal imagery won scores more. Among more skeptical and hesitant audiences she masterfully snared her listeners with a web artistically woven of parables, irony, metaphor, and satire. Her ability to weave these verbal and convincing webs was surpassed only by her ability to discern which particular mode would be most effective with her audience on any given occasion.

One day this Christian drew a blank among a group of seven men, who at that time were all involved in their trade as drug dealers. No matter what she preached, or how she preached it, their consciences remained seared and their hearts impenetrable. One of the men put this Christian on the defensive. "If I quit dealing," he asked, "will you provide formula for my baby, cover my wife's hospital bills, and pay our rent?" That Christian had forgotten that humans are economic beings. She now works for an accounting firm, experience that should prove helpful if she ever goes back to missionary work.

Once upon a time there was a Christian in the inner city who was a master networker and researcher of resources. He knew the service providers throughout his city by name and had gone to lunch with most of them. There could not possibly have been a resource of which he was unaware. He knew the ins and outs of securing federal, state, and local resources better than the legislators who introduced the bills to make such resources available. As one might guess, this knowledge enabled him to be a very effective witness in the inner city, where economic issues are at the fore. He explained to his parishioners that he was involved in the imitation of Christ, a major part of which is dealing with people as economic beings. The converts poured in, fast and fervently.

Although the number of converts increased, this Christian noticed that the conversions were sadly short-lived. Those for whom he secured economic help never took his help for granted and thanked him *ad nauseam*. Yet they quickly fell back into their old "vicestyle." To figure out where he had gone wrong, this Christian inquired of the parishioners themselves. What he learned is that nothing had changed in their lives except the ability to afford the lifestyle they had been living for years. Vicariously he heard the need for a support group to reinforce them in their efforts toward a new lifestyle. That Christian had forgotten that humans are social beings. He now works with problem-behavior children in an institution that emphasizes behavior modification. This should prove helpful if he ever returns to missionary work.

Once upon a time there was a Christian in the inner city who was very insightful and sensitive to the needs of humans as social beings. Aware of the pervasive loneliness in her community, she began many groups with regular gatherings, each designed to attract people with similar social needs in addition to intimacy. There were groups for new mothers, for example. These women shared helpful hints that eased the chore of child rearing, discussed the jealousy that their husbands exhibited toward a new member of the family, and so on. In another group for singles, a variety of issues were discussed, from budgeting to "safe sex." This particular Christian began eleven specialized groups. In each group she disseminated valuable and interesting information. The members of each group became normative checks for all other members. But what made the groups a success were the strong bonds of friendship so desperately needed by the participants.

The last I heard, these groups are still going strong, though the Christian is no longer a part of them. The friendship, love, and support they found among one another led to feelings of sadness, bitterness, and anger toward the people in their lives who had previously failed to supply these important needs. Even though this Christian pointed to Jesus as the epitome of friendship and the source of all fulfillment, group members tended toward self-aggrandizement. Reinforced among many of the group members was an unhealthy, selfish self-esteem readily encouraged and accepted in the "me" generation of today. In an attempt to regroup, the founding Christian is now enrolled in clinical pastoral education.

Once upon a time there was a Christian in the inner city who had just finished seminary, complete with an emphasis on clinical pastoral education. Aware of pent-up feelings, and being very adept at facilitating parishioners toward catharsis, this Christian set up a catchall group called "True Guts," appealing to, as he put it, the emphasis on toughness among those of lower socioeconomic status.

This Christian persuaded many of his parishioners that what really takes guts is being brave enough to become vulnerable to others. It takes fortitude to reveal the innermost thoughts of your heart and then to talk about how you *feel* about them. This Christian saw hardened criminals break down and cry, psychosomatic illnesses disappear, and a sense of release and relief never before known and enjoyed by so many in such communities.

The ministry was so successful that this Christian was able to start twenty-three chapters of "True Guts" in four communities. And it was ministry. One parishioner put it, "Now I know what the Bible means when it talks about 'putting off the old man'—

bitterness, envy, hatred, jealousy, anger. I know what the Bible means when it talks about the 'new man in Christ'—kindness, love, patience, joy, peace—real peace."

The last I heard, these groups, too, are still growing strong—though, again, the Christian is no longer a part of them. Not all the parishioners replaced the "old man" with the "new man." In too many cases negative emotions were not eradicated, but rather displaced. Children were neglected or given to foster care or adoption. Spouses were left or divorced. With negative feelings displaced, and without positive emotions given proper physical direction, the new emotions were directed toward other group members with whom parishioners successfully risked themselves. The physical expression of these emotions manifested itself in sexual affairs. The Christian had forgotten that humans are also physical beings. He is now studying psychiatry, which should prove helpful if he ever goes back to missionary work.

Similar scenarios could be drawn in the cases of Christians who deal with parishioners on an exclusively physical or cognitive level. The point should be clear. Successful Christian endeavors will take into account *all* of culture. By culture I mean "the totality of socially transmitted behavior patterns in people." The missionary endeavors of Jesus were holistic, taking into account humans as economic, social, emotional, physical, and cognitive beings. Even being present on earth, within culture, is a significant prophetic word. That word is that God is not interested in souls alone. Rather, God is interested in women and men as the cultural beings he created; he has not abandoned ship, and he has not lost sight of his original design or his intended role for people within it.

*   *   *

On one street corner in Chicago stands a beautiful church, so large that it takes up an entire city block. Apart from Sundays, one rarely sees people entering and leaving the church between 8:00 A.M. and 5:00 P.M. Before or after these hours one might biennially observe people entering or leaving this church.

On the corner directly across from this church is a McDonald's fast-food restaurant. This McDonald's is open 24 hours, 365 days a year. This particular McDonald's shows movies around the clock. For the cost of a small cup of coffee or soft drink, anyone can keep warm and be entertained for a minimum of two hours. Across the street some of the means of grace are securely locked behind heavy, beautiful oak doors. Other means are safely asleep on the top floors of skyscrapers or in the suburbs.

On which street corner is ministry being done? If your answer is "neither," that is no consolation for the church. Presence within a community is prophetic—not the presence of a church as a building, but as a people. Inner-city church buildings are often just another building to walk around at best; irrelevant, at worst. I am a firm believer in the gathering and communion of the saints in covenant with God. Just because community people know your building is a church and still do not come, to assume that they simply are not interested in a relationship with Jesus Christ is the height of arrogance.

Whoever made the rule that people must go to a church? Cannot community people with equal validity argue that if the church were interested in them, it would go to *them*? We need to be asking what the church, opening its building once or twice a week, is saying about God, the church, the parishioners.

The prophet's presence within a community is another way for a prophetic message to be conveyed. Jeremiah was present in the tribe of Benjamin. Not only was he present there, but Jeremiah also bought some land there and so by being present in this place he prophesied that houses, fields, and vineyards would again be bought in this land (Jer. 32:15). In other words, Jeremiah prophesied through his presence that reconciliation with God was still a possibility.

Micah prophesied to a community remarkably similar to a twentieth-century, North American inner-city community, a place where men lie in wait to shed blood, where the powerful call the shots, and where one's most dangerous enemies are one's own family. In the midst of all this, Micah established his presence as a prophecy of hope: "But as for me, I watch in hope for the Lord, I wait for God my Savior; my God will hear me" (Mic. 7:7).

*   *   *

Geographical places of presence are not the only places in which presence can mean prophecy. When a prophet takes his place among various populations, that in itself is a significant prophetic word. There is example after example of this in the ministries of Jesus and of the Old Testament minor prophets. In being with the poor, Amos, besides verbally prophesying against the rich with their misplaced ultimate concerns, is telling the poor that God has not forgotten them and is with them.

A Chicago police officer once said that the only people looking for runaway and homeless youth are pimps and pedophiles. He did not know about the Northside Ecumenical Night Ministry, of which I am a part. I am continually present among populations of homeless youth. That is only a third of the battle. The second third is establishing presence as we discussed in chapter 9. The final third is becoming a *prophetic* presence.

I hung out around Gaynelle and her friends for the longest time with no apparent prophetic progress. Our many hours of conversation were little more than superficial, or so I thought. Gaynelle was evidently in mental monologue with both them and my presence. She had to be in order to conclude what she did one day prior to her fatal overdose. On that day she declared to me, "God must have some plans for me or else there wouldn't be a Christian like you hanging around and wasting his time on me." By being present with this population of people, at least one homeless youth got the message that God was for her, too.

Lisa was among a population of females in prostitution with whom I hang around. She was the first of the women to talk to me. She spoke openly and honestly with me from the start. Given the depth of her guilt feelings, I could not comprehend how she lived under the burden of such guilt. Lisa was extremely bothered and depressed by her lifestyle. I offered her more resources than she could possibly have used. I offered to be with her and work with her in securing those resources. It soon became evident that physical needs were not her primary problem.

Lisa could not stand herself for what she was doing. She was punishing herself and considered herself undeserving and unworthy of any grace. I just kept hanging out, Lisa asking me the whole time how I could stand to be around "women like her." One day she got to the heart of the matter and asked what good could possibly come out of my associating with women like her. At that point I told Lisa the story about the prodigal daughter. When I finished, she gave me a hug, soaked my shoulders with tears, and said, "God doesn't just wait for his wayward children to return. When time is running out, he goes looking for them through people like you, doesn't he?"

In hanging out among gangs, the Christian's prophecy in presence is especially pointed. Although one would be foolish to directly challenge the supremacy of a gang on their own turf, the message the Christian gives by being there is a reminder that there is another Power that gives the Christian the fortitude to hang out on their turf.

After the Vicelord-Gaylord incident (see chapter 9), a couple of gang members grew curious about my courage and its source. I allowed their curiosity to stay intact. I answered their questions only partially and a few at a time. One week I told them I am a member of the "HCG." The next week I told them HCG stands for the "Holy Collar Gang." A couple of days later they insisted that if it was a real gang, the HCG would have an insignia. I borrowed their paint and painted a cross on the door of an abandoned building.

To this day I am slowly but surely satisfying their curiosity while whetting their appetite to join the most powerful gang alive in North America's inner cities. They cannot wait to learn more about the great HCG leader, whose wealth would have made Al Capone look like a pauper. I am certain most of them know what I am leading up to by now and consider it a game. But I am also certain that God can even use games, and the presence of a prophet who plays them, for the advancement of the city of God within the city of man.

*   *   *

Christians can also have a prophecy of presence in the specific places they frequent. Some of my favorites are restaurants, bars, and gamerooms. Whenever a Christian is present and recognized in public, he or she is a representative, a reminder, and a messenger.

Whenever I walk into a bar where there are some people who do not know me, prophecy is bound to occur. Seeing my collar, someone invariably asks what a Christian is doing in a bar or whether that is even allowed. Then they ask about drinking. I always say that there is nothing wrong with drinking in moderation. Even if they abuse alcohol and have no intentions of changing, they will say they are moderate drinkers and leave it at that.

When they ask whether or not I drink, things become a little more interesting. I answer casually and matter-of-factly, "No, I'm an alcoholic." If the questioner is an alcoholic, or thinks he might be one, I get a lot more questions to answer. I always emphasize that a person has to really *want* to quit drinking before it is even worth trying. A person needs to accept responsibility for his drinking and stop blaming other people or circumstances. If a person can do that, he is ready. Then I emphasize that no one can do it under his own power and that God is using Alcoholics Anonymous more than any other means for helping people to stay sober.

Judging by the numbers of people who have questioned me about being a Christian in a bar, I am sure there are scores of others to whom my cola-sipping presence has meant prophecy. I will never forget a reminder God allowed me to give at the Paper Nickle one night. After seeing me in this bar for weeks on end, Frank finally approached me to talk about it. "So, they let you guys out at night, huh? What else are you allowed to do?"

As our conversation progressed, it became apparent that Frank was struggling with what he considered to be irreconcilable differences between his alcoholism and his love for the church and desire to be actively involved in it. After a while he said that seeing me in the Paper Nickle from time to time got him to thinking that maybe God was saying that despite his hang-up with alcohol he could still be a church member. Frank concluded, "But I guess that's crazy thinking, huh?"

"On the contrary, Frank. I think your hunch is absolutely correct."

"You do?"

"Absolutely! In fact, Frank, in a sense your drinking problem is a necessary prerequisite to church membership."

"What on earth are you talking about, Father? If the church people knew I drink like I do, they would kick me out."

"Oh? Who do you think would be in a position to give you the first kick? The church is about people who realize that because of their sins they need the saving power that is available only in Jesus Christ. No one sin is greater than the others. If there is any difference at all between you and regular church members it is that you are more qualified than they for the salvation Jesus can provide. You don't have to be good enough to go to church. In a very real sense, you have to be bad enough."

"Wow! The way you explained that was just like a Sunday school teacher explained it to me in my teens. Now I know God was speaking to me when I saw you coming into this bar. I knew all that stuff. I had just forgotten it."

*   *   *

In this chapter we have considered the prophetic message inherent in the presence of a Christian as determined by various places of presence. However the Christian chooses to prophesy by presence, it must be a culturally holistic presence. A Gospel message that fails to take human culture into account, in whole or in part, is both ineffective and unbiblical. Prophetic presence within a community has to do with relevance, and among specific populations and at specific places, with particular aspects of the prophetic message. No matter where the Christian hangs out, the value of her presence as prophetic is dependent on the way in which the Christian is present. That is the concern of chapter 11.

Modes of Presence

Prophetic messages lie in the very mode that the prophet chooses to express his presence. One's style can be active or passive, imperious or receptive, verbal or illustrative, stringent or flexible, agitating or serene. The Christian can be a lecturer or a listener, an ally or an avenger, a friend or a foe, a boon or a boot.

One needs to look closely to discern a difference in style from prophet to prophet within the Old Testament account. With few noticeable exceptions, the prophets appear to be active, verbal, imperious, stringent, and agitating. Upon closer examination, however, one is able to detect some differences in style. Jeremiah exhibits a remarkable sensitivity and depth of feeling. As noted earlier, Hosea is fervently patriotic and a warm humanitarian. Under close scrutiny one is able to detect in Nahum's harsh and seemingly cold prophecy characteristics that are consonant with the meaning of his name, "comfort" or "compassion."

If these prophets lack evidence that, in addition to their

utterances, their presence was also prophetic, the reader should bear in mind that, just as the net result of their verbal proclamations was seldom recorded, how much less likely that of their personal lives and proclamation of presence. It is also possible, given the historical context, that verbal prophecy was the most effective form of prophecy in that day. That still does not eliminate the evidence, albeit limited, of their prophetic presence, and this fact cannot be used to deduce that prophecy must always be primarily verbal.

Jesus prophesied with cultural means and, except for the periodic miracle, according to cultural limitations. Jesus did not oppose culture. Where there was dissonance, Jesus was working on the transformation of culture, not its abolition. But in another sense, Jesus' prophetic presence was transcultural; Jesus ignored man-imposed classifications and ranks. His eyes did not distinguish between female and male, free and slave (or any other socioeconomic status), Greek and Jew. And Jesus was colorblind to the various shades of people's skin.

The contemporary inner-city Christian must operate in this same transcultural mode if God is going to be able to prophesy through her. Sexism, racism, and any other kind of prejudice is a stumbling block and unquestionably sinful. A transcultural presence is in itself prophetic. The proclamation is that God is a God for all people, everywhere, regardless. . . .

With a transcultural mode of presence, females in prostitution will accept the male Christian's presence in puzzled delight. They are befuddled because most or all other males have treated them as property. The fact that you do not mind, or at least will tolerate, sitting on a soiled and sunken couch in a roach-infested cubicle-of-an-apartment will do more to soften the stony heart of a poor person than any amount of verbiage. To eat the raw fish of the Japanese, the chitterlings (hog guts) of blacks, or the denogoan (meat cooked in pig's blood) of the Filipinos is more convincing of the prophet's relevance to a particular race or culture than any amount of Scripture quotation.

*   *   *

In prophesying through presence, sometimes the appropriate style can be determined only when one is in actual contact with parishioners. Various styles will be appropriate, depending on the cultural background, personality, and immediate circumstances of the parishioners. When in doubt, I encourage a "laid back" or serene style.

For too long, inner-city residents have experienced the insensitive and disrespectful onslaught of evangelists who not only invite themselves into other's homes, but without a second thought prop their feet up on the coffee table. I am talking about people who shout out the way of salvation without regard to the circumstances of others—circumstances that may make giving such a message at that moment inconvenient or even irrelevant. I am talking about those who present the heart of the Gospel in a threatening way and figuratively hit people over the head with a Bible. We must show others the respect that is inherent in agape love. God asks us to be a prophetic presence, not a present "pain in the ass."

So far I have provided examples of the *via negativa*. Here I wish to illustrate how a passive and serene, nonthreatening and respectful style will not only enhance one's presence as a prophet, but make it possible in the first place.

I met Jackie, an eighteen-year-old mother, in November 1986. I talked to Jackie only twice in November, but learned that she had to give up her child to a foster parent. Jackie was sad about that, even though her mother was the foster parent. Although I do not know the exact reason why Jackie had to give up the child, I do know that the reasons were legal and somehow related to her recent divorce. By her words and her actions, I could tell that Jackie was both sad and depressed.

After I hadn't seen her for more than two weeks, Jackie suddenly showed up on a seat next to me in the Agathos Eatery. We exchanged greetings and a couple of minutes went by, when suddenly Jackie accused me of staring at her hands. I did not think much of it at that point. A couple of minutes later, however, she asked, "Why do you keep staring at my hands?" Then a "light bulb" went on for me and I said, "You must be feeling awfully guilty about something, Jackie."

That was the crowbar toward catharsis. "Oh, I am!" Jackie cried. "I feel awful about what I've done. Just look at my hands!" Now I could see "tracks" (rows of tiny scabs resulting from hypodermic needle injections) and knew for certain what I had suspected from nearly the start of our conversation. Jackie was injecting drugs. To avoid sounding threatening or judgmental— which Jackie appeared to be afraid of in the first place, and which I feel would only have alienated her from any possible help I might give—I casually asked her why she did not inject in the veins just underneath the elbow as most drug-users do.

After her explanation that she had no veins suitable for the job in that place, we were able to talk at length about things to live for and reasons not to give up. Jackie seemed to feel better just talking about it. I judged that her use of drugs, although serious, was more of a symptom than the cause of her problems. After discussing some options with her, I referred her to a Christian organization with small-group therapy, which I have since learned has served Jackie well.

*   *   *

As a listener, the inner-city Christian fulfills some roles of the prophet. I said earlier that prophecy is a word from God to his people. Listening, too, is a word from God. Under certain circumstances verbal prophecy can be misinterpreted to mean, "God wants you to know where he is at and what he is thinking, irrespective of where you are at and what you are thinking." In the prophecy of presence, and especially in the mode of a listening prophet, the representation, reminder, and message are about a God who is willing to hear a person out, to dialogue, to interact, to reciprocate, and—despite the grief this might cause God—to be a friend.

Friendship through listening is a good place to start. It has the potential to open up many doors, including the one that leads to eternal life. Despite the overpopulation of the inner cities, inner-city people are very lonely. Nearly everyone is out and about solely for self-interest and self-gain. Manipulators abound, and the art of manipulation grows daily in the varieties of form and levels of skill. It has gotten to the point where everyone trusts no one.

Christians are not immune to distrust. Because of the modes of presence exhibited by some evangelists and missionaries, they are often perceived to be less trustworthy than others. They have shown themselves not to be above manipulation and enlightened self-interest. For those Christians who are able to establish presence, they will find eager recipients of prophecy that comes from a listening mode of presence.

With few if any friends who will provide unconditional listening time, parishioners are laden with thoughts and feelings, joys and concerns which, unless they are able to unload them, will drive them to despair, insanity, or worse. Without fail, when I am on the streets or present at specific places, just by virtue of the fact that I am present in a serene and listening mode of prophecy, the stories people need to tell and the emotions they need to express seem to involuntarily fall from their mouths.

I had just settled into a booth in a Lawrence Street bar one day, when a woman of Mexican descent sat down across the table from me and said, without my knowing so much as her name, "Big problems. Long time. My husband he no make love to me no more." On the street, in front of the Agathos Eatery, a young man spent all of five minutes sizing me up. Seeing the acceptance I had among the others present, he approached me and burst into tears saying, "My mother said I can't go to her wedding. She said I'll attend over her dead body. She shouldn't tempt me like that."

*   *   *

Modeling is another mode of presence in which the missionary is powerfully prophetic. How the Christian behaves shows what God expects of people. I walked by a group of men one night and was going to keep going, but they began to ask questions. With the exception of one person, they were curious what a minister was doing in such a bad neighborhood, especially at such a dangerous time of night. The one exception was a very drunk and belligerent man. He began to swear at me and accuse me of being a false prophet, so to speak. We continued to talk in between this man's outbursts. His friends told him to "shut up" and show a little respect. We talked some more. Then the drunk man began jabbing his index finger against my clerical collar and accusing me of all manner of vileness I cannot even imagine, let alone be guilty of. His friends physically restrained him, and we tried to talk some more. At this point the man was trying his best to get to me, and I was feeling very unsafe.

I was also angry. In all honesty, I was so angry that if no one else had been around I might have very likely punched him out. As it is, I was "Mr. Cool." I calmly told the fellows that I enjoyed talking to them very much, that I was sure we would see each other around, that we could have a good chat then, but that under the circumstances it would be best if I moved on for the time being.

Two days later I saw three of the men again, and we talked pleasantly. They apologized for their friend. Then one of them thanked me. "For?" I asked. "Well," he replied, "it is incomprehensible to me how you were able to walk away the other night. I could tell you were angry, and your pride had to take a beating. Yet you walked away, and that taught me something very important. It taught me that God will give me the strength to do right as long as I really want to." I am in doubt about the strength I had, but God did arrange the circumstances in such a way that I chose for the right and thus could be an effective prophetic model.

Gerry, a thirty-six-year-old woman, was lying on a snow bank unable to get up. She yelled for help to get on her feet, but none of the scores of people around were even tempted to help Gerry. After I helped her to her feet, it was obvious that she also needed help getting to her apartment. She was too inebriated to balance two steps in a row. I all but carried her the four blocks to her apartment.

The apartment complex in which Gerry lived was notorious for the extensive drug dealing that goes on in and around it. As we neared the complex, a couple of fellows tried to sell some marijuana and cocaine to me before they noticed my collar. One, although apparently embarrassed, said, "Well, ya never know!" They were not making it any easier for me to decide whether or not to bring Gerry all the way to the fourth floor.

To make things worse, I knew that the elevator in the building seldom worked. If it wasn't working, there was little chance that Gerry could make it up the narrow and winding stairwell by herself. But I decided that Gerry's chances of being raped or freezing to death outside were greater than my chances of being assaulted inside. We entered the lobby. The facial expressions of two women and a man in the lobby exhibited shame at the sight of me escorting Gerry. At the time I didn't understand why.

Thank God, the elevator worked. Unfortunately I did not know how to work it. It could very well have been the first elevator ever invented. As I was moving around trying to figure it out, I lost my hold on Gerry, and she fell to the floor. I picked her up again, and then one of the women in the lobby volunteered to "drive" for me. That was a special blessing. I was not about to go inside Gerry's apartment, but this woman did and laid Gerry down on her bed.

Back in the lobby I spent some time talking with the two women and the one man. Before our conversation got under way, however, a couple of guys came in from outside. One of them said, "We were timin' how long it took you to get that woman into her apartment, preacher. You must be legit. You didn't have time enough to take advantage of her." One of the three with whom I spoke in the lobby said it was a shame that an outsider had to take care of their own. Another said, "But I guess someone who has God is never an outsider, right?" Bingo! To five more people (possibly six, if Gerry remembered anything the next day), God allowed me to prophesy, to model, to show what God expects of his people.

*   *   *

The final prophetic mode that I wish to discuss is immediate advocacy. Advocacy in general involves the kingly role of the missionary (see part 4). By immediate advocacy I mean on-the-spot, short-term help that makes life at least a little more tolerable for a parishioner. Sometimes this is nothing more than a phrase of encouragement or a question, the answer to which, although obvious, is necessary to lead the parishioner to a more hopeful understanding of a situation about which he has a narrow, cluttered, or clouded view. At other times immediate advocacy is more extensive but less direct. I will illustrate each.

Our paths crossed when he was at his wit's end. For days he had been mulling over a decision for a dilemma in which he saw only two possible solutions. His problem regarded gangs and school. For the last two weeks some gang members had been threatening him on the way to and from school. The Friday before the weekend that I met him, the gang had given him an ultimatum: Join the gang on Monday or die. The gang succeeded in making him see the choices along their lines.

This young man's parents heavily emphasized school. If he did poorly in school he faced a punishment almost as severe as that threatened by the gang members. And he really did wish to please his parents of his own accord as well. But he couldn't think of any alternatives—all he thought the whole weekend was, "I've either got to join the gang so I can do well in school, or else I have to quit school." After he explained the situation to me in detail, I asked the kid, "Would it be possible for you to take public transportation or get a family member to take you to school?" At that point his eyes brightened, a smile spread across his face, and he said, "Yeah! Why didn't I even think to go straight to my parents with the problem? Thanks, Rev!"

Another incident involves my colleague, Rev. Peter Brick. After establishing presence with Trena, Peter learned that she had been homeless for two years in five different states. She had been sleeping in unlocked cars, dumpsters, and abandoned buildings. As Peter got to know Trena better and better it appeared more and more miraculous that Trena ever would have trusted him. Several times during her homelessness she had gone to various social work organizations when her situation became desperate. Each time, against her wishes, social workers attempted to contact her parents. Trena was terrified at the prospect of having to see her father again. He was extremely abusive, and Trena was sure that if she ever ran into him again, he would kill her.

That explains Trena's very first words to Peter: "You're a minister, right? Which means that no matter what I tell you, you won't repeat it without my permission, right?" With that out of the way, their relationship developed quickly and firmly. Trena would often call Peter in the afternoon to set up a time when and where she could count on seeing him in the evening. There never seemed to be any specific reasons why Trena wanted to see Peter. When they met on the streets, they just took long walks and Trena talked Peter's legs off.

After a time Peter was able to put the pieces together. Trena always wanted to see Peter at 10:00 P.M. on weekdays and at 11:00 P.M. on weekends. Those were the curfew hours. Without an adult around after these hours, Trena had to live and act like an adult and live in worry of being found out by the police. As long as Peter was around she could act her age, forget her cares for a while, and live carefree. Peter was glad to advocate on Trena's behalf in this manner until better circumstances could be secured.

*   *   *

The inner-city missionary has the privilege of being a prophet of God. Inner-city ministry has its difficulties and discouragements, but overall it is enjoyable. This privilege, challenge, and enjoyment is available to all Christians who are willing to commit a little time to the inner city and who wish to make a difference. With guardian angels all around and forgiveness for the asking when we err, we can have a grand time being bold, innovative, and creative in our prophetic work in the name of God. The success that this creates in bringing inner-city parishioners to seek out the Christian in her priestly role is the subject of part 3.

Part Three

VISIBILITY: The Priestly Role

The confessor will most likely awaken the next morning and ask herself, "How drunk were you? You really believe you saw a minister in a bar?" Or back to her normal emotional state, she will be angry with herself for expressing remorse and regret over sins she wishes she had not divulged.

As he explained his need for prayer, he too began to cry. He begged for prayer so loudly that the entire bar heard what was going on. Before I knew it, I had three people kissing me, two people hugging me, and four people holding my hands—all nine of them crying and begging for prayer and blessings.

I have prepared and preached a one-sentence sermon to many one-time visitors to the more vice-ridden sections of the inner city: "Where one hangs out in life is often a big factor in determining where one ends up in life."

Chapter 12

On Shepherding

Acting out a prophetic presence is, for the Christian, a ministerial role. As ministers we are to be "servants of Christ, and stewards of the mysteries of God" (1 Cor. 4:1 NASB). Then, once our prophetic presence is established, we become inescapably visible, which expands our role to that of a priest or pastor. As pastors we are imitators of "the great shepherd of the sheep" (Heb. 13:20).

Psalm 23 is a beautiful analogy of our relationship to God—we are to God as sheep are to a shepherd. But there is a basic flaw in the analogy; not in the psalm itself, but in its usefulness in explaining the shepherding role of the inner-city Christian. In David's psalm the sheep has all kinds of needs and gets in all manner of trouble, and the shepherd takes care of everything. In that way the psalm accurately reflects the stupidity and helplessness of sheep. But the "sheep" in Psalm 23 is actually a cognizant being who claims and clings to his shepherd. Real sheep do not know enough to do that.

In the inner city the Christian must fulfill her priestly role in the full sense of the shepherd analogy, acting out her role as a shepherd whether the sheep like it or not. One of these priestly roles is restraining those who err. In fulfilling this role the inner-city shepherd should be of this mind: "I am your shepherd; you shall lack nothing. I make you to lie down in green pastures, I lead you beside quiet water, I restore your soul. I guide you in paths of righteousness for his name's sake" (based on Ps. 23:1–3).

*   *   *

When I met Carlos, he still lived at home. He was seventeen years old and had just graduated from high school. After I had gained some rapport with him, I asked Carlos whether he felt the streets of Uptown were a good place for him to hang out. Carlos said it was important for him to be streetwise because he did not know how long his folks would let him "live off them." "You shall lack nothing," I thought, and I prayed.

Carlos had given up on job hunting before he even began. I gave him three referrals. He followed up on one of them, finished a pre-employment program, a job training program, and is now working full-time. Carlos works at a 7-11 store for little better than minimum wage, but he is self-sufficient, happy, and hopeful. The last time I spoke with him, Carlos said, "You watch, I'll be managing that store in a year or two." Since Carlos began job training, I have not seen him out on the streets. I made him "to lie down in green pastures."

One night as I hung out in front of the Indian Trail Saloon, a forty-three-year-old mother came walking down the street in a drunken stupor. Just before she entered the Indian Trail, her ten-year-old son, who was tagging along behind her, said, "Mom, I'm not going into another bar!" In they went. In I went. I began small talk with mother and son. Soon mom was off and fighting.

I asked the boy if he knew how to read.

"No."

I asked if he had a father.

"Yes, he doesn't drink so much like Mom."

I then gave him my Night Ministry card, which listed several help hotlines, including one for Alcoholics Anonymous and another for detoxification centers. I told the boy to show his dad the card and tell him to get help for his mom's drinking problem. He replied, "Yeah, Mom threw up blood last night." If the card was not enough to convince the father to help his wife, maybe it was enough for him to keep his boy out of the bars. I have seen his mother in the bars since then, but the boy has not been with her. I would like to think I was instrumental in leading the boy out of bars and "beside quiet waters."

On Montrose Street I met a group of teenage parents. They were naturally curious as to what a minister was doing out so late, so I introduced myself and showed them one of my cards. One teenager noticed a parental stress hotline and asked about the quality of the operators. As our conversation progressed, it became apparent that this parent was under a great deal of stress. Even though he needed the break, he felt guilty about being out, having a good time without his children, and doing something for himself. He obviously did not err by neglecting his children, but he did err in the opposite extreme.

We talked about his three children for quite some time. He had delightful stories to tell about his children, and it was obvious that he loved them abundantly. As he spoke I interjected statements of support, encouragement, and reassurance. Finally I spoke at length about the work, burden, and fatigue involved in child rearing. I eloquently swung into my "sermon" on how, if a parent does not take enough time for himself, he is in a very real sense a bad parent. The children become irritable. The parent becomes irritable. Things are said in the heat or exhaustion of the moment that may be detrimental to the child's emotional health and development, and so on.

"Therefore," I said in conclusion, "you are a good parent. You have given yourself a much-needed break. You will go home refreshed and renewed and much better able to realize your full potential as a caring, nurturing, loving parent." More questions followed on the topic of coping. I enumerated some alternative measures and one compromise measure. I told him that if he just could not get over his need to always be doing something for the children, he might consider joining a support group for parents. That way he would get some time out and still be helping his children. I hope I have in some way served to "restore his soul."

* * *

In fulfilling the priestly role of restraining those who err in the inner city, the Christian must often be aggressively passive. At times this happens naturally by virtue of visibility alone. I have mentioned before how often I see guilt written on the faces of parishioners when I walk down the street or enter bars. Admittedly, this usually has a very temporary restraining effect. But my visibility has led several parishioners to a complete turnabout with respect to at least one aspect of their lives.

In dealing with alcoholics and problem drinkers it is especially important to be aggressively passive. Weekly, without fail, I am approached in a bar by someone under the influence who pours his heart out to me, confessing alcohol abuse and a desire to escape drunkenness, but a lack of willpower to do so. Invariably I give them a card and tell them to call me the next day. That may sound cold and unfeeling, but feeling is just the point.

Under the influence of alcohol, expressed emotions, although real, are exaggerated and often involuntarily expressed. The confessor will most likely awaken the next morning and ask herself, "How drunk were you? You really believe you saw a minister in a bar?" Or back to her normal emotional state, she will be angry with herself for expressing remorse and regret over sins she wished she had not divulged. I've even had people become angry with me and blame me for manipulating them while they were under the influence. The short end of it is that you cannot reason with or minister to a person under the influence. Do not waste your time "throwing pearls to swine." If they are not swine, they will get back to you.

The passive approach is still the best way to handle those who do wish to get off drugs or alcohol. Passivity does not exclude toughness; rather, it is crucial to "tough love." Remind the parishioner that the problem is hers, not yours. Then find out why the parishioner wants to quit. If it is for any reason other than herself, forget it. I have gone that route myself. I went to Alcoholics Anonymous for God, for my wife, for Mom and Dad, for any and every reason except for myself, and I still drank until *I* wanted to quit.

There is more respect for Christians in this day and age than one might guess. Giving the "cold shoulder" sometimes will shock the parishioner just enough to get him thinking seriously. When you put the responsibility in the parishioners' laps, you help them become aware of their own latent power to control their environment rather than be controlled by it.

The Christian's visibility as an abstainer within the bars is in itself quite an eye-opener to many. Renee stared at me in disbelief. She stared at me to the point that I became most uncomfortable. I left for another bar. Renee followed and stared at me in that one too. To two more bars Renee followed me. Finally I asked her what she was doing.

"You always have more fun than I do, and you don't even drink," she said. "I'm sorry if I've made you uncomfortable, but I just had to find out your secret."

"Well," I said, "I believe everyone has got to be high on something in order to really be happy."

"But you don't drink. What are you high on?" Renee asked.

"I'm high on showing people that life can be fun without an artificial high."

"*I'm* trippin'!" Renee exclaimed. "You're high on Jesus, aren't you!"

"You said it."

*   *   *

I have prepared and preached a one-sentence sermon to many one-time visitors to the more vice-ridden sections of the inner city:

"Where one hangs out in life is often a big factor in determining where one ends up in life." Only God knows the outcome of those messages. But because so many to whom I have preached this sermon have never been seen by me again, I am hopeful. In restraining those who err, the goal is reconciliation with God in Christ. The above illustrations give no examples of that goal having been reached. Only Jesus himself can ensure that. All we can do is lead the sheep. Toward that end I have led the sheep by restraint of those who err, but it is God who must corral them. I have guided parishioners in "paths of righteousness for his name's sake," but only God knows how many of these have entered his fold.

Chapter 13

It's Jesus' Fault

The priestly role of a Christian is also to comfort those who are in distress. In fulfilling this role the inner-city shepherd should be of this mind: "Even though you walk through the valley of the shadow of death, you will fear no evil, for I am with you; my rod and my staff, they comfort you" (based on Ps. 23:4).

*   *   *

"I know you're a minister," Sherrie declared. "I've seen you around and seen you help others." We talked for quite a while before Sherrie mustered the courage to tell me what was on her mind. Transferred from her thoughts to her tongue, Sherrie's burden suddenly spewed out. Time and time again she had gone to drug and alcohol rehabilitation centers only to buckle under severe peer pressure when she came back to live in her community. "Try as I might, pray as I might, I just can't do any better in this community," Sherrie cried in distress.

I arranged for Sherrie to be admitted to a rehabilitation program one more time on the condition that I be allowed to do follow-up work with her. She agreed. The follow-up consisted of meetings during peak times of peer pressure. In these meetings we engaged in catharsis exercises. I also reviewed alternative approaches and attitudes toward peer pressure with Sherrie.

"Is it more frightening to say yes or to say no to your friends when offered drugs?"

"It is more frightening to say no," Sherrie responded.

"Then which decision requires more bravery?" I asked.

"It takes a lot more courage to say no."

"Are you a brave person, Sherrie?"

"Yes."

"As a matter of fact, you are very proud about how brave a person you are, aren't you, Sherrie?"

"Yes, I am."

"Then all you need to do is show it in yet one more way."

"You're a cool dealer, Rev. I'll give it a shot."

Sherrie proved herself equal to the task. With each new day and each new victory, I reinforced her. As time progressed we also began to talk about replacing bad habits with good ones by turning her negative past into a positive future. We honed Sherrie's gifts of self-sharing. Experienced with addiction, she is a very effective counselor and is currently working on credentials to counsel professionally. When I first met Sherrie she cried that she couldn't do better in her setting. Now she declares that she can't do better than by working in her setting (even though she "walks through the valley of the shadow of death").

In my priestly role I deal with many cases that are not at all unique to the inner city. Laurie lost a loved one, William was hospitalized, Franco had an accident, Julio had an apartment warming, and Ross got married. It is the circumstances surrounding these cases, however, that make them unique and so trying to the inner-city Christian. Laurie's husband was bludgeoned to death on Christmas day, William was hospitalized because he jumped off a tall building under the influence of Superman and is now paralyzed from the waist down, Franco had an accident when he missed the person he was attempting to run over and drove his car through a storefront, Julio had an apartment warming because he was kicked out of his parents' home, and Ross got married to Richard.

Nevertheless, my *form* of pastoral care isn't unique just because I work in the inner city. Visible as I am, inner-city people still look to me to fulfill my priestly function on their behalf. A pedophile called me at my office to tell me Laurie's husband had been killed; William's best friend asked me to visit William in the hospital; Franco asked me to visit him in jail; Julio's brother told me about Julio getting kicked out of the house; and Ross asked me to officiate at his wedding. Even though I am unable to honor all their requests, my parishioners know that I am with them and look to my rod and my staff to comfort them.

*   *   *

Visibility in my priestly role fills a need in the inner city that I never dreamed existed anywhere. When I reflected on various attitudes toward God, I used to classify them as either positive or neutral. However, the inner city seethes with negative feelings toward God that are often expressed in anger. My visibility provides a target, a tangible image of God, toward which many direct their anger. Like a sponge, I soak up the anger that has been trapped inside of so many people for so long.

While I was walking along Racine Street one evening, a guy began spitting at me. After several attempts he still had no score. Just when I thought he had retreated to the locker room, he began following me, still intent on spitting at me. I ran around the other side of a parked car and stared over it at the angriest face I have ever seen. He began cursing: "---- God. ---- God, dammit. Damn! Damn him!" He ran over to the car and tried to spit on me twice more. I ducked the first shot and sidestepped the second.

His anger was too fierce to extinguish verbally, and I wanted to avoid physical restraint. I figured my only hope was to redirect his anger. "It's none of my business," I said as calmly as I could, "but it seems to me that if you are mad at God, you ought to go spit on him. I am merely his ambassador. Or perhaps you would allow me to take a doggy bag of spittle to him." Besides saving my own skin, I also hoped for the remote possibility that the man would see how ridiculously he was behaving and want to dialogue in a more customary manner. Instead he laughed insanely and left.

In another incident, I walked into a bar, and a woman whom I had never met before in my life began crying hysterically and screaming, "If your God is a God of love, how come he let my eight-month-old baby die when, after five long years of trying, I finally conceived?" I told her I wasn't sure and asked if we could talk about it. We talked for an hour and a half. I said no more than twenty words—words such as: "Um, uh-huh . . . How shattering . . . You sound angry . . . Are you serious? . . . Um, pain. . . ."

There was, of course, no way I could ever have satisfactorily answered her question. Her immediate need, and the need of scores of others like her with whom I come into contact all too frequently, is a need that can be filled only by a Christian who is visible in the priestly role. She needed access to God to tell him how angry she was with him. I brought her to the altar. I put her in a position such that she knew God had heard her complaint. Her anger may still have been great enough to make the line of communication between her and God tortuous and obscure, but enough of it was removed to allow once again for a word from God.

The good Lord gave me "a rod and a staff" to comfort the parishioners he has entrusted to my care. Sometimes the valley of the shadow of death through which they walk is incredibly dismal. I do not always know what to do or to say so that they may know they need not fear any evil. Yet somehow God uses my visibility as a shepherd-priest to provide comfort. I am humbled when, despite myself, others are comforted—only God knows how. The following are some examples of such incidents:

Priest: Whoa, Lucky! What happened to you?
Lucky: Three assholes beat the hell out of me on my way
         home from work last night and stole my paycheck.

Priest: That's deep, babe.
Lucky: I'm tellin' ya. Now I have a face a man won't
         look at 'cuz it's beat to hell, I don't know how I'll
         feed my daughter, and I got hospital bills to pay.

José: Rev, hey Rev! Wait up!
Priest: What's up, José?
José: You know my brother "Slick"?
Priest: Yeah.
José: Well, he told me you could maybe help me.
Priest: Lay it on me.
José: I'm eighteen, right? No one will let an eighteen-
         year-old sign a lease or even rent a room in one
         of those cheap hotels for transients. . . . No, man.
         My mom moved out of town. I just got no place
         to go, man!

Susan: What ya been up to, Mark?
Priest: Oh, I visited Rock in jail today.
Susan: Oh, you do that too? How is she? . . . Well, you
         don't suppose you could visit my sister Tina in jail
         too, do you? . . . That'd be great, but no, I can't
         go. I was an accessory to her crime.

Priest: What's up, Roslana?
Roslana: Nothin' to it.
Priest: Keep out of trouble, hear?
Roslana: Trouble . . . well, there is one thing, Mark. I've
         got to appear in court for a prostitution rap.
Priest: Need a lawyer?
Roslana: No, I've got a lawyer. But it's still scary. I'm only
         sixteen and they want to try me as an adult.

Priest: Hi, Tim.
Tim: Oh, hi, Father. Savin' any souls?
Priest: You tell me.

Tim: Father, I'm not into religion really. Although I do
           believe there's a God. But could you possibly help
           me with something else?
Priest: That's what I'm here for, Tim.
Tim: I'm afraid I might have VD.
Priest: Have you seen a doctor?
Tim: I don't have any parents, at least who'd claim me,
           and I'm not on General Assistance.
Priest: There are free clinics.
Tim: Father, I'm only fifteen. If I go in, you know
           they're under obligation to call the police.

Only because I was visible in my priestly role as a missionary
did the parishioners involved in these incidents confide in me.
Because they confided in me with an understanding of my priestly
function, they were comforted in knowing that God, too, had heard
their pleas.

*   *   *

McBeth always seemed depressed and never smiled. True, his
sin was great, but unlike so many others, he did not seem able to get
over it. McBeth had allowed himself to be hired for arson, and two
jobs went well. But not everyone escaped from the third building he
torched; two children died. One child died from smoke inhalation;
the other burned to death. McBeth saw their anguished little faces
just before they died. That would have been enough to depress
some of the most sociopathic people. But McBeth had gone
through the grieving process, so I thought that something else had
to be troubling him.

McBeth had paid heavy penalties and had been incarcerated for
seventeen years. His experience in jail could almost make death look
inviting. Still, as I observed McBeth from day to day, it was
apparent that he did not feel that he had paid enough. He thrived
on self-flagellation. I just kept being his friend and hoped that one
day he would allow someone to help him. He had become a
Christian in jail, but the joy of Christ somehow escaped him.

One day as we were talking, McBeth let loose. No longer able to bear the load of his guilt, he unleashed the hell that had been trapped inside of him for so long. "Death, death, death!" McBeth screamed. "I am deserving of nothing but death!" I had never before talked openly with McBeth about the deaths he was responsible for. Now I asked him to recount the story for me in detail.

At first McBeth vehemently refused to go back in time and review the tortured faces of his two youthful victims. After nearly another hour of vacillation between stone silence and more cries of anguish, I told McBeth that he needed to meet his victims face to face if he was ever to be able to bury them once and for all.

Finally McBeth gave in. Although his verbal recollection took only minutes, it seemed like hours. When he had finished, I asked McBeth to take one more very close mental look at the faces of the two victims of the fire.

"Do you see them?" I asked.

"I do," said McBeth.

"Do you see them as clearly as ever?"

"Yes!" McBeth screamed, even more anguished.

"Good! Listen, and listen very carefully. The death of those two children before you now . . .

"Yes?"

" . . . is Jesus' fault!"

In the silence that followed I prayed fervently that McBeth would understand. Praise God, he *did* understand. Once again McBeth cried like a baby. But this time he hugged me and let himself be hugged. This time the tears of McBeth fell across lips parted in a smile as he cried, "It is . . . it is . . . praise God, it *is* Jesus' fault!"

*   *   *

Providing parishioners with comfort is a weighty task. The inner-city Christian must always bear in mind the difference between fulfilling this role in the inner city as opposed to fulfilling this role in most other settings. In the inner city those who need comfort the most are the least likely to pursue it. Simply by making herself visible as a priest, however, the inner-city Christian almost automatically draws those to herself who need a word or action of comfort. Supplemented with prayer, the provision of such comfort can often be evangelistic. This priestly function of intercession is the topic of chapter 14.

Barroom Bawl

In the priestly role of intercession the Christian must first pray for himself. Then he must pray for others. Sometimes parishioners will ask you to pray for them, although this seldom occurs in the inner city. If they don't request prayer for themselves, it is sometimes appropriate to ask parishioners if you may pray with them. Whether praying for or with parishioners, the inner-city Christian must be of this mind: "I prepare a table before you in the presence of your enemies. I anoint your head with oil and your cup overflows" (based on Ps. 23:5).

*   *   *

I dare not go anywhere without first praying. We depend on God for safety at all times, everywhere. But prayer for the inner-city missionary takes on new importance. In the inner city we enter a land where Satan has his greatest foothold; a land filled with people literally possessed by some of the devil's minions, some who have lost control of their minds due to drugs, and others who in the desperation of their poverty will not hesitate to kill to survive.

In addition to physical safety, it is important to pray for emotional and professional safety, wisdom, guidance, and discernment. As well-trained, well-equipped, and well-prepared as the Christian may be, it is all for nought if she does not know how, when, and where to apply her skills. Needless to say, even then, only by God's work through the Christian will her labors bear fruit.

It is also important to pray for the parishioners before one leaves the home or office. My prayers for parishioners before working among them always include two essential petitions. First, I pray that God will lead those who need him most to cross paths with me and that the door to conversation and help will be open. Second, I pray that God will soften the stony hearts of parishioners whom I have known for some time but who remain withdrawn and uninterested in either verbal or service evangelism. Both petitions have paid divine dividends.

At the Liftland Hotel there was a young man, Doug, who sold drugs full time. The almighty dollar was his only concern. He sold drugs to young people and continually worked on getting them hooked on the more deadly drugs because they brought higher profits. Doug also recruited young people to sell drugs for him. Even Doug's fourteen-year-old brother, "Face," was pushing drugs for him.

Doug tolerated my presence as long as it was fleeting. My visibility meant nothing to him. Daily I prayed that God might soften his stony heart. As usual, God worked through circumstances. Doug's brother got thrown into jail for possession of narcotics. When I learned about the plight of Face, I immediately suspected that God had his hand in this.

Finding Doug, I expressed my sorrow and concern and said I would do what I could to visit Face. Doug was very happy about the interest I took in his brother. Then, as I was about to walk away, Doug's tough image cracked and he broke down and cried. Admitting his responsibility for their dilemma, Doug asked me to help both of them get back on the right track. Doug's heart was softening; the door to ministering to him and discipling him opened.

It is also important to pray continually. Even while among parishioners I am praying. No matter how adept I am at establishing my presence among my inner-city parishioners, no matter what my visibility means to them, it is all in vain if God is not at work as well. So as I walk down the street and see Martel inebriated again, I pray, "O Lord, may his hangover tomorrow be severe enough for him to at least entertain the thought that he might need professional help for his addiction." As I see Mick hassling the "winos," I pray that he too might be hassled enough to let me tell him about foster care and transitional living programs and other alternative living arrangements that will lead him away from the lifestyle of those he mocks.

Often I am praying even as I am talking with a parishioner. Of course, that prayer can be for myself: "Lord, this fella doesn't look like he's gonna take no for an answer. Chill him out, please!" When I pray on behalf of the parishioner, I pray for her understanding of a certain concept, her belief in my sincerity, her openness to considering an alternative; or strength for her to endure, courage for her to maintain, hope sufficient for her to continue.

Sometimes God honors my request so quickly I do not realize he has already acted. When I do notice an immediately honored request, I am often not ready for it. Like the maddeningly slow government workers who determine the eligibility of my parishioners for General Assistance, somewhere along the line I got the idea that God always takes his own sweet time in answering prayer, especially if the answer is yes. But no matter what the answer is or when it comes, we must not forget to follow up with prayers of praise and thanksgiving.

Because of my visibility in the priestly role, people encountering me often instinctively ask me to pray for them. Many people still harbor the old notion that a minister's prayer is somehow more efficacious than their own. On a few occasions when someone has asked me to pray on his behalf, I assured him that I would, but also reminded him that he has equal access to God and that he also should bring his concerns to God. In some cases the parishioner simply could not believe that his own prayers could do any good.

I suppose someday I will meet a parishioner with whom I would press the issue. But for now, when I pray for someone, I ask him to pray for himself as well, but I do not insist on it. Forcing a parishioner to pray has only done harm. Two parishioners whom I pushed into prayer haven't spoken with me since and believe, as one of them put it, "If you were truly a representative of God you would *know* that God had put you in a special position for intercession." Although incomplete, her perspective is accurate.

The disadvantage of not insisting that parishioners always pray for themselves is that some are left in their ignorant belief that my prayer is magical. I know such beliefs exist because of those who also ask me to bless them. For similar reasons I do not argue about this issue either. Part of my task as a priest is to pray and to bless people. By acceding to their requests for prayer and blessing, I keep the door open for future ministry.

I also continue in my role as a praying, blessing priest because at times my prayer or blessing causes the parishioners to behave differently. Their behavior becomes a "self-fulfilling prophecy." Who is to say that God is not worthy of the credit despite the fact that we can understand the phenomenon psychologically. The parishioner himself does not hesitate to attribute the outcome to the workings of God made efficacious through my prayer or blessing.

I do, without fail, press one issue among my parishioners about prayer. That issue is summarized by the ancient Latin phrase, *ora et labora,* prayer and work. A common contemporary way of saying this is, "The Lord helps those who learn to help themselves."

Dillon was one parishioner for whom this approach was particularly meaningful. He asked me to pray that he would get a job, since his estranged wife wouldn't return until he had one. I told Dillon that if he would get pre-employment training I would pray that the job openings would come and that his wife would live up to her part of the bargain. It took four-and-a-half months, but he did the work and the prayer requests were answered in the affirmative. Dillon is now preaching *ora et labora* to others.

*   *   *

In only my second week with the Night Ministry I entered the Paper Nickle bar. An American Indian woman in her early fifties asked me to pray for her. "I'll be sure and do that," I promised. She hugged me and bowed her head. Trying to put her off, I said, "Yeah, my wife and I have devotions every night, and we will certainly remember you in our prayers." Beginning to cry, she declared that she needed prayer immediately.

Soon a friend of the woman came over and requested prayer also. As he explained his need for prayer, he too began to cry. He begged for prayer so loudly that the entire bar heard what was going on. Before I knew it, I had three people kissing me, two people hugging me, and four people holding my hands—all nine of them crying and begging for prayer and blessings.

Needless to say, I was more than a little uncomfortable and self-conscious. But at that point their very lives depended on me. One needed blessing because she could barely tolerate her present life situation. A few others echoed those sentiments. Another requested prayer to carry her through her grief. Others needed prayer because of their guilt.

All these barroom parishioners believed that in the midst of life, their common enemy, I could "prepare a table before them." I did so. In God's name I blessed each one of them. I "anointed their heads with oil." And "their cups overflowed" in a flood of joyful tears that replaced the tears of guilt, grief, and distress. What I had feared doing had become inevitable; in fact, my *fear* of praying now seemed more out of place than the praying itself.

In the presence of their enemy I prepared this table before them: "Gracious God in heaven, our enemies are numerous, our guilt is great, our distress is unbearable. We know that you understand because you experienced all the temptations, grief, despair, and pain that we experience when you came to live among us through your son Jesus Christ. In the midst of a place where there are so many barroom brawls, we are in the midst of a barroom bawl because we know we can count on you. In Jesus' name, amen."

Chapter 15

Moccasins

To fulfill the priestly role a Christian must sympathize with weakness (Heb. 4:15) and deal gently with those who are ignorant and going astray (Heb. 5:2). In doing so, the inner-city Christian should keep this in mind: "Surely goodness and love may follow you all the days of your life, and you may dwell in the house of the Lord forever" (based on Ps. 23:6).

* * *

For months Etta talked about murdering her husband. Few took her seriously, including me. When she was herself, Etta was as kind as could be. But on drugs she became controversial and violent. When she was herself, her husband beat her terribly. When she was on drugs, Etta's husband found her behavior entertaining. When she was herself, Etta loved her husband despite his beatings. When on drugs, she wanted to kill him. It was while she was on drugs that Etta stabbed her husband twice through the heart.

I went to see Etta in jail. She did not remember me because she had always seen me while she was on drugs. I asked if I could do anything for her, and she wanted me to pray for her husband, not knowing that he had died. When I broke the news, Etta cried. "What is to become of me?" she sobbed. I knew she meant it in a spiritual sense. "If you allow him to," I said, "God can show you that he is bigger than all this. A criminal hung on a cross next to Jesus and was invited to heaven just minutes before he died. It's never too late."

The first time I met Cole he almost hurt me badly. Bent over with his hands near the ground, Cole held an aluminum can in each hand and was banging them together and chanting nonsense in a very loud voice. When I approached him, Cole jumped up and took a swipe at the side of my head with one of those jagged-edged aluminum cans. I blocked his shot, and he ran off laughing like a hyena.

The deinstitutionalization of the mentally ill that began in the mid-1970s let loose a lot of "Coles" to run around Uptown. Their illness is a type of ignorance that most Christians, including myself, cannot begin to understand. What I do know is that Cole and others like him understand friendship and love. I usually express my love to these parishioners with hugs. Having dealt gently with the "Coles," I cling to the promises of God for mercy and love on their behalf.

Helen never did believe I was a minister. One night she was thrown in jail for assault and battery, and if it had been left up to me, I would have let her stay there. She couldn't just disbelieve my ministerial credentials and leave it at that; she had to hassle and harass me too. But I had been given divine orders to deal gently with the ignorant and straying since I myself was subject to weakness (Heb. 5:2).

So I went to the jail and asked Helen if I could do anything for her. She asked me to contact some people who would help raise the bail. None of them was willing to contribute. When I went back to the jail to give Helen the dismal report, the sergeant said to Helen, "Since this minister shows such interest in you, I'll let you go."

Helen asked why I even bothered with her when she was so mean to me all the time. I replied, "I did the same thing when I was your age." Perhaps anger is to hurt as hate is to murder.

As I was walking along Sheridan Street near Leland, I saw a girl attempting to attract customers for sex. She got my attention because she was very young and also because I could tell she was inexperienced. I figured she had a pimp because she knew enough to hang out by a bus stop so that it would look to the police as if she was merely waiting for a bus. I lingered, hoping for the opportunity to strike up a conversation with her.

It was twelve degrees outside so I soon retreated to a fast-food restaurant to sip coffee and observe from there. Later the girl also entered the restaurant. It soon became apparent who her pimp was. He allowed her to warm up a while, then asked her to go out on the street again. She complained that it was too cold and it probably would not pay off on such a cold night. He still insisted that she go outside.

To get into conversation with the pimp, who was black, I put on my black voice and said, "You cold bro!"

"You see it everyday, Father," he responded, "You see it everyday."

I then got up and sat down in a booth next to him. He declared that he was not such a bad guy, that he took good care of his four girls, that he did not force any of them to do what they do.

"I'll say one thing for you," I replied, "You're picking up a lot of slack left by the government and the area churches."

*   *   *

On an urban playground known as "The Mall" I met an Indian from the tribe of the Seminoles. She was sniffing talley (the street name for glue). I asked her about the advisability of her behavior. She replied it is wonderful anesthesia for the oppressed and it is appropriately priced.

At that point I went into a long homily about how things are never as bad as they seem and tomorrow is another day and there are other recourses and oodles of resources and so on. When I was finished I thought I had done pretty well. But all she said in reply was, "Have you ever heard a saying something about walking a mile in someone else's moccasins?"

Empathy is certainly in order. In his priestly role Jesus is the greatest of all empathizers: "For we do not have a high priest who is unable to sympathize with our weaknesses, but we have one who has been tempted in every way, just as we are—yet was without sin" (Heb. 4:15 NIV). Surely goodness and love can follow our ignorant and straying parishioners all the days of their lives, and they can dwell in the house of the Lord forever.

Some parishioners will close their ears to the Word verbalized. We must deal gently with them and be empathetic. Perhaps when they sense our empathy, our parishioners will open themselves to the Word experienced. They can experience God's Word if we properly fulfill our kingly role as missionaries. That is the topic of part 4.

Part Four
AVAILABILITY: The Kingly Role

Rather than evading and retreating in the face of Satan's work, I face it head on like a jiu-jitsu warrior, turning the strength and the force of the attacker against himself. I make "deacons" out of his pimps, pedophiles, and drug dealers.

Because he felt it necessary to overstep the bounds of his authority, it became necessary for me to assert mine. "Officer!" I shouted. "We do not tolerate that type of behavior in our neighborhood, and I know your commander doesn't either!"

Part Four

AVAILABILITY: The Kingly Role

Chapter 16

Establishing the Church Council

"I went on a walk today."

"That's good."

"No, that's bad. I fell and sprained my ankle."

"That's bad."

"No, that's good. Where I fell I found a hundred dollar bill."

"That's good."

"No, that's bad. When I reached for it, I was bitten by a bug."

"That's bad."

"No, that's good. In jerking my hand away I uncovered two more hundred dollar bills."

"That's good."

"No, that's bad. I was then arrested on suspicion of robbery."

*   *   *

So much of life is merely a matter of perspective. For too long Christians have viewed life from too narrow a perspective. A proposition, a situation, an occurrence is termed either lightness or darkness, positive or negative, good or bad.

Worse than our categorizations, however, is how our categories cause us to react rather than act. We isolate ourselves from propositions, situations, and occurrences that are dark, negative, or bad.

"A pimp is bad, that is all I need to know, now I will stay away."

"A bar is bad, that is all I need to know, now I will stay away."

"A slut is bad, that is all I need to know, now I will stay away."

Such narrow-mindedness is certainly comfortable. With a proposition, situation, or occurrence labeled as bad, I no longer need to think about it or deal with it. I am in the right. That is all I need to know and that is all that matters. But such a perspective gives us a distorted view and understanding of reality. This dichotomous view of life fails to see that pimping and drug dealing and prostitution are economic issues as well as spiritual issues. The dichotomous outlook denies any self-responsibility. In writing bars off as bad places, one becomes smug and secure, if not self-righteous, in knowing that he does not go there. This is especially comfortable because he will never have to consider the possibility that perhaps a bar provides a legitimate human need that his church fails to provide.

Worst of all, this attitude denies that God's sovereignty extends over all of life. Can any proposition, situation, or occurrence in life be so bad that we should stamp it as "evil" and declared off-limits—so that even God himself is cut off from it? The Bible abounds with examples of God using that which was intended for evil to his own advantage, glory, and honor. God is in total control over every sphere of life. As one of my parishioners put it, "The devil ain't got nothin' comin.'"

Perhaps this unbiblical dichotomy explains why our church buildings look totally irrelevant in our culture. At best our church buildings look anachronistic; at worst they seem opposed to culture. Jesus' life and ministry did not at all exhibit the "us against them" mentality so prevalent among Christians today. Jesus' mentality was that of kingship; he promoted his sovereignty in all areas of life. He strove to transform culture, and he expects no less from us.

As a street minister who specializes in outreach to homeless youth, I meet many pimps who have homeless girls working for them. I could easily write them off as evil people and leave it at that. But that does them, the girls, me, the church, and God no good. God has asked me to transform culture, not stand in judgment of it. God wants me to work toward the realization of the city of God within the city of man.

I have taken on a more Christlike, king/queen-like, role as a Christian. Rather than evading and retreating in the face of Satan's work, I face it head on like a jiu-jitsu warrior, turning the strength and the force of the attacker against himself. One of my more systematic ways of using the devil's work against him is by turning the work of his employees to God's advantage. I make "deacons" out of his pimps, pedophiles, and drug dealers. I make "elders" out of his bartenders and gang leaders. Through them I am more readily available to my parishioners.

Deacon Don is a pedophile. His intentions are evil—the sexual use of young boys. As long as the boys are willing, he will have sex with them. But common grace also has a hold on Don. He is concerned for the boys' well-being, wanting them to get help and do better for themselves than a life of prostitution.

In this latter respect, Don is a deacon. He provides for the boys by hooking them up with me. Don is very well-informed and knows the details of every youth in prostitution. Without Don it would take months of hanging out for me to learn names, origins, history, and other details. As I hang around with Don some nights, he will point to a kid and say, for example, "You probably haven't seen him before. His name is Danny. He came here from Minneapolis two weeks ago. He's fifteen. Danny came to Chicago fleeing an abusive stepfather. For a place to stay he exchanges sex with the last 'trick' of the night for a bed to sleep in. He's presently the 'hottest' boy on the strip."

When he feels a boy will be open to it, Don directly introduces me to him. The boys see my acceptance of Don as a person and thus are more likely to seek my friendship. I must not fail to add that I also have a genuine friendship with Don. He fully understands and accepts my agenda. No manipulation is involved. Under these conditions I do not think God has any qualms with my accepting the groundwork information and introductions that I glean from the work of the devil through Don.

Deaconess Flora is a drug dealer. Her primary hangout is the urban playground called "The Mall." Flora knows everyone within a four-block radius of the Mall. Because of the nature of her business, it took a very long time for me to gain Flora's trust. Now she too knows what I do, respects it, and encourages it.

Like Don, Flora aids in my knowledge of and introduction to others, drug users or not. Whereas Don helps me to work among a specific population, Flora helps me to break down my exegesis of the community of Uptown into a more specific exegesis of a neighborhood within the community. Flora works in a neighborhood filled with poor southern whites.

I have often wondered why there is such a large number of southern whites in the inner cities. I have much more to learn, but Flora taught me that many of the southern whites come from very poor southern communities like Cary, Mississippi, or from the countryside shacks that abound in many southern states. They are latecomers following the example of blacks who came to the industrial North decades earlier seeking better employment opportunities. Needless to say, such opportunities no longer abound, but these southern whites are by and large still much better off.

With this help from Flora, my ministry in this neighborhood has flourished. Minimally, I have the tolerance of the entire neighborhood. When I am consulted for help, my detailed exegesis of this neighborhood, made possible by Flora, has made me more available in the sense that I have a framework within which I am better able to gain trust, understand, empathize, counsel, and make referrals. Flora's profession is evil. Despite it, because of Flora, the city of God has a foothold on some more real estate within the city of man.

Jerry is a person who pimps. The first few times I watched him relate to his employees, as open-minded and nonjudgmental as I like to think I am, I nearly regurgitated. How could I ever befriend someone engaged in such immoral and disgusting work? For the longest time I could not. I have had these feelings for all my deacons at one time or another, and only through fervent prayer and God's help am I able to get beyond the person's attributes and profession to the person himself.

These feelings were particularly strong with respect to Jerry. I am not one to spiritualize matters quickly, but in this case I am only able to understand it spiritually. Because Jerry has been by far my most helpful deacon, I sincerely believe Satan himself was working to thwart any understanding or relationship between Jerry and me. I also believe that God intervened because it was Jerry, not me, who initiated contact and cultivated our friendship.

Jerry has been most helpful for two reasons. First, he is in touch with ports of entry for homeless youth from out of state. He freely shares with me the locale and dynamics of those ports of entry. And Jerry does have a lot of kindness in him. Previously, when homeless girls did not want to work for him, he felt bad that he knew of no alternatives for them. He said he often could not sleep at night, remembering the face of a young kid and not knowing what would become of her. Now Jerry is very pleased and proud that he can refer them to me.

More recently our relationship and friendship has grown to the point that Jerry has also agreed to refer to me any of his current employees if they ever want to get out of "hustling." I am praying for the day when he will actually encourage that. In the meantime, I thank God for Deacon Jerry. Despite the occupation, the person has made me more accessible to my parishioners.

*   *   *

In addition to "deacons," I presently have three categories of "elders." I distinguish between deacons and elders according to their level of commitment. My elders are store owners, bartenders, and gang leaders. Some of our elders have actually been committed enough to attend seminars held by the Night Ministry to teach them skills in empathetic listening, needs discernment, and the like.

Andrus is an elder who runs a "greasy spoon" located on a particularly seedy and dangerous street in Uptown. He has made his restaurant available to me as a place of refuge. In turn, this allows me to be much more available to the parishioners on this street.

Andrus is also a very insightful person. Nightly I take a break from my street ventures and over a cup of coffee engage him in both delightful and helpful conversations. Andrus has taught me a great deal about how various lifestyles, attitudes, and vices are related to socialization, economics, and politics. This has broadened my perspective on how to be more specifically available.

Bartenders who accept eldership always prove to be helpful. They are glad to have Christians in their bars to help relieve them of their caseloads. Whether they like it or not, bartenders must listen to the gripes of what at times must seem like the entire community. Bartenders are more aware than most people of the depths of a person's heart. They are also the hub of neighborhood information, hearing all the gossip and taking and giving more messages than most small-town switchboard operators.

It was Elder Gus who tipped me off to Cara's need for help. Cara was thirteen years old. She entered Gus's bar every day after school to buy a pop. Because Cara attended school faithfully, it took Gus a long time to discover that there was something wrong with her. He knew Cara's parents were poor as paupers. It finally dawned on him that there was no way Cara's parents could afford something as impractical and unnutritional as pop every day.

Gus began asking Cara pointed questions. Cara was very nervous in answering, and some of her answers were unquestionably inaccurate. Gus began noticing other strange characteristics about Cara but, as he put it, he couldn't "put his finger on it." At last Gus apprised me of the situation and asked me to check it out.

It took me a while to figure Cara out too. In a lot of ways her behavior and mannerisms resembled those of a homeless, teenage prostitute. Yet I knew Cara was not homeless. School was going very well for her. She was never out past curfew, she never missed school, and she always did her homework. What did tip me off was that, in addition to buying pop, Cara could somehow afford to go into the gameroom every day.

After hanging out in the gameroom. I discovered both the source of her income and her problem. Cara never missed school. Cara got good grades. Cara was always home by curfew. But between the time the 2:45 school bell rang and curfew, Cara was fellating males in the gameroom for a dollar per customer.

I had to deal very carefully with this situation. If I went directly to the school authorities or to her parents, I would lose all credibility among the homeless youth and other youths at risk of homelessness. The word would be out in a day that "you can't trust that man in the collar." In this case I called on a social worker to "blow the whistle." But my availability was made possible in the first place because of Elder Gus.

*   *   *

A couple of gang leaders have proven to be helpful elders. I was talking to a store owner/elder about how I wished to make inroads as a Christian on Maynerd Street. He told me about a Latin King gang leader through whom I might try to work. "Introduce yourself to him," he instructed, "and tell him what you are about. If he talks to you, you are in. If he walks away, get out of there."

This gang leader goes by the street name "Bandit." If you ever had a stereotype of how a gang leader looks, talks, and acts, he fits it. But Bandit opened up to me right away. He showed me every tattoo (I think) on his body. That venture alone took forty-five minutes and was Bandit's way of being open and intimate. He told me about his experiences in the "big pen"—the penitentiary. Bandit showed me slash and burn and bullet scars.

Before meeting Bandit I knew a lot about gangs. I knew their colors, emblems, signals, and lingoes. I knew their alliances and foes; their destruction and brutality. From Bandit, however, I gained an insight to which very few are privy. As we walked down the street, Bandit pointed to some homes with signs in the windows that said: NEIGHBORHOOD WATCH AREA. WE CALL THE POLICE. "How can they do that to us?" Bandit asked. "After all the Kings have done to protect this area, safeguard these people, and look out for their children, this is the thanks we get!"

This taught me that not all gang people consider themselves bad or unwanted by the larger society. They perceive that their function is accepted and appreciated. Because my reasons for seeking acceptance in the neighborhood were in accord with the Latin Kings' self-appointed mandate, their leader readily accepted me. Various gangs do engage in illicit activities. But it is justifiable, even honorable, in their eyes if it is done for the good of their neighborhood—their turf. It is a revived Robin Hood syndrome. I have never met anyone as altruistic as Bandit. He loves his turf so much that he is prepared to die for it.

In a very real sense, Bandit calls the shots in his neighborhood. On the same day that I first visited him, he put the word out all over the neighborhood, "Don't mess with the Rev. Defend him under any circumstances. Feel free to go to him for help with anything." In the months that followed, I was swamped with neighborhood people, young and old, coming for anything from counseling to questions about the Bible to advice about what kind of car to buy. The last time I was on Maynerd Street, an eleven-year-old asked me for a calling card to give to a friend because Bandit said I was real good at helping kids and her friend had a real mean mom.

*   *   *

In establishing the church council, the inner-city Christian makes herself available to parishioners. To be available is to give the city of God a foothold within the city of man. Even within an adversary kingdom such as that of the Latin Kings, the Christian is able to recruit deacons and elders to serve the purposes of the kingdom of God. This should not be too surprising—we know, after all, which king and which kingdom are sovereign.

Chapter 17

Bedfellows

A common contemporary saying has it that "politics and religion make strange bedfellows." For the inner-city Christian who wishes to make a difference, these two are necessary bedfellows. Establishing one's availability does no good if one is unable. Because Christ is king we have the confidence to struggle fearlessly against the devil, sin, and death. Christ is the protector and defender of his church; under his leadership we can battle fearlessly.

Running around yelling "injustice" at the discovery of abused, homeless, or hungry people helps no one. We cannot merely demand better in the name of Christ. Although such declarations and demands are true and legitimate, they do not provide food, shelter, or medical attention. In feeding the five thousand, Jesus began with the fish and bread already available. By becoming involved in politics, the inner-city Christian begins with what is already available. God has ordained governments to serve and protect, and it is through them that we must first work for justice.

113

Getting involved in political action groups, government-sponsored education, and training groups, the Christian becomes more available to her parishioners on three very important levels. First, the Christian will know and understand the laws, making it easier to help parishioners know what they have a right to expect and claim. Second, the Christian can act on the parishioners' behalf to push for new laws where protection and services are lacking. Third, the Christian gains the power of legal knowledge and the power of connections to legal and other professional persons, many of whom are also involved in political pressure groups. Again, the Christian's availability and clout are strengthened, enabling her to claim rights on behalf of her parishioners.

*   *   *

In the state of Illinois, eighteen-to-twenty-year-olds are in a type of legal limbo. They are old enough to vote and serve in the armed forces, but not old enough to sign a lease. Because of age they have passed out of the substitute care system, but are ineligible to receive adult services. The legal difficulties of this age group are further complicated by a misunderstanding of their rights, which is a direct result of this legal ambiguity. Thus potential service providers who are ill-informed and in fear of liabilities take the attitude "when in doubt, deny services."

The Night Ministry has worked hard at clarifying the legal rights of this age group. We are disseminating our findings to other service providers. Our biggest task recently has been to persuade shelter providers that it is legal to shelter people in this age range. This is especially important because of the lack of legal right to sign leases.

One evening three of my parishioners were arrested for assault and battery. All three were minors—one fifteen, two sixteen. More than five hours later, two of them were back on the streets. I asked them where Harriet was, and they informed me she was still in jail because she needed to come up with a fifty-dollar bond. Something was wrong, for a minor does not need to pay bail; instead, a minor's parents are notified and the youth is released upon their arrival. Furthermore, it is illegal to hold a minor for more than six hours.

At the lockup the sergeant explained that Harriet was seventeen and therefore liable to be tried as an adult and must go bail. I concluded that I must have been mistaken about Harriet's age. I asked Harriet if I could do anything for her, and she requested that I contact some of her friends on the street and see if they would collect the fifty dollars she needed for release.

Harriet's friends all refused to help bail her out because they said she was sixteen—a minor—and therefore should have called her mother to be released. I realized then that Harriet had used false identification. Whereas I had earlier felt a responsibility to Harriet, now I felt a responsibility to the police. If they took her to the county jail they could be sued heavily for incarcerating a minor at that facility.

Returning to the lockup, I told the sergeant about it. At first he panicked. I had informed him that Harriet had two previous arrests, that the youth commander would recognize her, and that she had used false identification. The sergeant checked the records, not thinking that Harriet could use a false name in addition to a false age. He could find nothing, but he released her "on her own recognizance"—a step that I took to mean he was protecting himself just in case.

Because I knew the legal issues involved, I had felt a ministerial duty to the police department. While bringing Harriet home I learned that her two previous arrests were as a juvenile but under different names. After these arrests she acquired a seventeen-year-old's identification because her mother would not tolerate a third arrest. At that point my responsibility shifted from legal to ecclesiastical. She confided to me as a minister, and her testimony to me remains confidential.

*   *   *

It used to be that public aid—General Assistance (GA)—in Illinois could not be obtained by anyone not having a permanent residence. That does not make too much sense since people without a permanent residence are often homeless and those most in need of GA. The law was recently changed at the urging of those of us who belong to political action groups. The particular group with which the Night Ministry is most closely associated is the Youth Committee of the Chicago Coalition for the Homeless. Now GA checks can be sent to currency exchanges, hotels, and churches.

Much more needs to be done. The criteria by which eighteen-to-twenty-year-olds are deemed to be eligible are too formidable. One criterion is proof of independence. Such proof is usually verified by means of a rent receipt, so many homeless youth are still unable to get GA. The Night Ministry staff is handling this in two ways. We are directly helping people in this age range who are indeed eligible to prove it. We are also working with the Youth Committee to change the eligibility criteria to more reasonable standards.

The most important legislation recently passed in Illinois in regard to homeless youth is a bill called "Minors Requiring Authoritative Intervention," or MRAI. This law is good in that it removes criminal status from young people who run away from home. It is also a good law in that *in theory* it allows minors to obtain services without necessarily having to be reunited with an abusive family.

What is bad is that in practice the law emphasizes family reunification even when there is evidence of an abusive home life. Family reunification is always best where there can be love, acceptance, and reconciliation. But the state operates with the understanding that, in the opinion of voters and taxpayers, family reunification is best, period. Because of that pressure, MRAI is being abused by people who discourage homeless youth from going through the process of obtaining much-needed social, medical, and legal services.

I know of a sixteen-year-old, for example, who is the mother of a fourteen-month-old child. Because of an intolerable situation at home, she ran away with her baby. I referred her to a social agency that agreed to help her obtain services through the MRAI process.

At the police station, where all MRAI processes must begin, a state caseworker who prided himself on his record of family reunification told the girl that she could pursue MRAI but also warned her that she would lose custody of her baby. Discouraged, the girl went home. The caseworker got another check mark for the admiration of his employer. Meanwhile, nothing at home had changed, so the girl left her baby and ran away again.

Because the MRAI process begins inside a police station, I must work within its ramifications when I counsel homeless youth. In the first place, I must do my part to seek a change in the law. As it is, most homeless minors would rather earn money through vice than obtain services through a process that threatens reunification with an abusive family. Unfortunately I must be the one to warn them of the risk involved in obtaining services through the MRAI process. In chapter 18, I address a third option.

The inner-city Christian should take advantage of the many government programs available. Designed to educate and train community leaders, these programs can equip the Christian with skills and knowledge that will make him more available to his parishioners. Such programs have included sex-education clinics, seminars on how to detect and deal with gang activities, and drug education.

My most recent training has been in AIDS education. I am now a certified AIDS counselor. Because of the widespread misinformation and consequent panic about AIDS, I owe it to my parishioners to be well-informed. Like it or not, it is my job as a Christian to provide certain knowledge about the AIDS disease and to comfort not only the AIDS victim, but his family and other community members who daily live in an unrealistic fear of contracting the disease. Given the complexity of the moral issues involved, I believe it is my Christian duty to be available and able to inform others about "safe sex" practices or about sterilization measures for hypodermic needles.

*   *   *

Nothing disheartens me more than the legal issues surrounding housing. The laws are so complex and the loopholes so many, it is nearly impossible to distinguish between one's right and one's privilege. I had to learn all about these matters when I worked with the Roseland Christian Ministries Center on the south side of Chicago.

What I have found is, directly or indirectly, the result of governmental policy toward the poor. Absentee landlords neglect rental property, bleeding tenants for as much as they can get. If landlords do make improvements, then property assessments and, therefore, rents increase. Meanwhile, tenants who are ignorant, irresponsible, or psychologically handicapped abuse and damage the rental property.

"Red-lining" is a well-known phenomenon in which financial institutions designate areas for which they do not want to grant loans. They dodge laws against this practice by requiring higher down payments than for comparable housing elsewhere in the city. They also charge higher-than-usual interest rates and loans for housing that is beyond a certain age. Finally, they stall on getting appraisals, hoping people will be discouraged and go elsewhere.

The problem of abandonment naturally occurs in slum areas. Cities have tough housing codes and tough penalties for owners who fall short. It would cost the landlord a great deal to bring a residence up to code, and in a lot of cases a renter would ruin it in a year anyway. So no money is spent on it, no taxes are paid, and court hearings are delayed for two to three years. In the meantime the landlord milks the tenant for all he is worth. When the landlord finally appears in court, the judge threatens to seize the property, and the owner says, "Go ahead." This whole process is known as "dead-ending."

"Urban homesteading" is a program designed by the government to get property that was seized from negligent landlords back into the hands of a private citizen and restored to livable conditions. The program stipulates that the new owner pay a nominal price of between five and twenty dollars to obtain the property. The property must then be rehabilitated to meet all the city codes, and the new owner must live in it at least five years before selling it.

The problems with the urban homesteading program are insurmountable. The property is usually so deteriorated by the time the city acquires it that it cannot be rehabilitated. Or if rehabilitation is possible, it is so costly to bring a house up to code that only the rich can afford to do so. The owner must have skills in remodeling, electrical work, and plumbing to make it worthwhile. Frequently these properties are in areas with high crime rates.

It takes the city a long time to acquire or tear down a building. First the city must find the owner—a formidable task in itself. Once found, the owner is given sixty to ninety days to fix up a property. If he does not comply, he is given sixty to ninety days to tear it down. If he still does not comply, the city takes it over and gives a wrecking crew sixty to ninety days to tear it down. The whole process frequently takes years. The last I heard, it costs the taxpayers between $9,000 and $10,000 for one home to be torn down in the city of Chicago.

More recently I have been trying to understand how politics is related to the growing scarcity of single-room-occupancy hotels (SROs). Through the process of "gentrification" of neighborhoods, SROs are rapidly decreasing in number. Gentrification is the term given to the recent trend toward revitalizing old housing and hotels in central cities by turning it into residences for the affluent, such as condominiums, thereby displacing the poor who lived there. With the decrease in SROs comes an increase in the number of homeless people. At times ten inexpensive rooms for the inner-city poor are turned into one luxury apartment for the wealthy.

*   *   *

Obviously, even the most energetic of inner-city Christians cannot keep abreast of the political scene in its entirety along with taking care of other domestic and job-related responsibilities. We must choose which issues to get involved in and which to pass by.

Our choice should conform to our parishioners' greatest needs and our own particular gifts, interests, and abilities.

If we have a general understanding of the laws and are pushing for new laws where the old ones are ineffective or inadequate, and if our parishioners are still not getting what is theirs by right, then we may have to resort to yelling "injustice" and demanding better for our parishioners in the name of Christ. We also may have to break "Sabbath laws" in order to fulfill our queenly/kingly role as inner-city Christians. That is the subject of chapter 18.

Walking Tall

Having networked with all the major service providers in the inner city, having a thorough grasp of all the major legal issues, having the support of influential leaders from nearly every sector of the city; and most important, having been called and commissioned by the King himself to work in conjunction with his kingly role, we can now walk tall. Walking tall is the act of confidently fulfilling one's queenly/kingly role in Christ.

As I walked around the corner of the Liftland Hotel I came upon a police officer lecturing four of my teenage parishioners. The officer saw me, but ignored me. He snapped at the teenagers, "Forget his collar! Forget my badge! I kicked ass when I was six for a pack of cigarettes, I kicked ass when I was sixteen, and I will continue to kick ass around here as long as the business people will pay me off with cigarettes to keep you kids from loitering around here."

As long as the policeman was all talk, I had no problem with him. I did not need to lower myself to his level and engage in a power struggle to prove my manhood or test my authority against his. If he had a need to feel more powerful than a minister, I would do what I could to help him get over his insecurity. But this officer could not just verbalize his threats and leave it at that.

Perhaps because the kids showed no fear, the officer felt it necessary to grab one of them and violently pin him against a rough brick wall. Because he felt it necessary to overstep the bounds of his authority, it became necessary for me to assert mine. "Officer!" I shouted. "We do not tolerate that type of behavior in our neighborhood, and I know your commander doesn't either!" The policeman immediately let go of the kid and left.

*   *   *

In early October I met a man named Kent in the Paper Nickle at about 10:00 P.M. Kent was on crutches. He was not drinking alcoholic beverages; he had a job and wasn't going hungry. For these reasons I was confused when he entered the bar and said he was specifically looking for me at the suggestion of a parishioner. As it turned out, Kent had been suddenly evicted from his apartment. He had no money until he got paid at the end of the next day, he had absolutely nowhere to go, and it was very cold for early October.

No shelters open in Chicago before the first of November. All the neighborhood SROs were full, and I did not have the money to put Kent up in a nicer hotel. I made a few calls to the hotlines for the homeless, to no avail. Finally I took Kent to my office, where we enjoyed some coffee while I spent no less than an hour and a half on the phone trying to find a place for him to stay that night. I turned up absolutely nothing.

As we sipped our coffee and chatted, I suddenly had a brainstorm. "Say, Kent, how good an actor are you?" As one would expect, Kent looked puzzled. "I mean, could you come off as a drunk if you had to?" Kent thought he could do a pretty decent job, but wondered what that had to do with a place to stay for the night.

I proposed that we go to the local liquor store, buy a bottle of beer, spill some on his hair and clothes, and have him chug-a-lug the rest.

If Kent smelled and acted like a drunk, I thought, we could get him admitted for the night into the YMCA detoxification facilities. Kent performed admirably. He pretended to fall off his crutches a couple of times, and he burped in the face of the admissions counselor. I even commented, "You've got to stop doing this to yourself, Kent; you're gonna end up breaking that other leg too." Of course, my collar didn't hurt our cause any. Kent was accepted immediately.

My colleague, Rev. Peter Brick, met Lucan, a homeless boy of sixteen. Lucan had been homeless two-and-a-half years and during those years had lived in more than a half-dozen states. It took Peter a lot of patience and hanging out for a long time before Lucan finally gained the courage to speak to him. When he did speak to Peter, he asked, "You're a minister, so I can trust you not to tell anything I don't want you to, right?" With that established, Lucan slowly but surely opened up.

After a time Lucan told Peter he desperately needed some medical attention. Peter explained the MRAI process, but it soon became apparent that this was out of the question for Lucan. He was unable to trust social workers, let alone the police. Lucan had been arrested on charges of prostitution twice previously. He was already a ward of the state, but had run away from his foster parents, who abused him just as his natural parents had. Lucan was not yet willing to try transitional living program alternatives.

Since the MRAI process necessarily begins in a police station, since the government provided no alternatives, and since Lucan himself was not ready for any of the private options, Peter secured medical attention for Lucan illegally. I had previously worked out an agreement with a medical facility that was willing to serve homeless youth for whom MRAI is not an option. Peter gratefully took advantage of this networking on Lucan's behalf.

Lucan was understandably quite nervous entering this medical facility. He asked Peter to watch the phones. "If the police are called, I do not care at what stage of the examination I am in, come into the examination room and get me out of here," Lucan commanded. All went well. Like us, the medical personnel at this particular facility feel that, although our primary strategy must be to get laws changed that deny the basic rights of our parishioners, until such changes are in place, it is still our responsibility to do our part in fulfilling the kingly role of Christ, regardless. . . .

*   *   *

In fulfilling the queenly/kingly role to which we are called by Christ, the inner-city Christian must be available as Jesus was—on the parishioners' turf. Along with our presence and visibility, our availability on the parishioners' turf is a particularly potent evangelistic method and message which affirms that God is alive and well and at work in his world.

Part Five

GROWING DEEPER:
In Deductive Retrospect

Just as "the Sabbath was made for man and not man for the Sabbath," so too the Bible was made for man and not man for the Bible.

When we must decide how best to present the Gospel to others, it is, I contend, as equally valid for one to figure "when in doubt, try it" as it is to deduce "when in doubt, don't risk it."

Chapter 19

One Message, One Vision

In the four New Testament Gospels, a basic unity in the Gospel message of each writer confronts and challenges readers with Jesus Christ. Yet the different emphases in each Gospel enrich the readers in their understanding of Jesus Christ. The Gospel writers purposely selected parts of Jesus' deeds and sayings according to the effect they wished to achieve.

In other words, given the targeted recipients of their testimony, each Gospel writer chose those deeds and sayings of Jesus that he believed would best strengthen faith in Jesus and his mission. The contents and emphases in each Gospel were determined by the mindset, philosophy, and needs of each audience. Each Gospel writer was concerned with this question: How can the one and only true Gospel message be presented in such a way that it is good news to these people at this point in their lives?

Matthew, who wrote with the Jews in mind, records 606 of Mark's 661 verses. But Matthew does not simply reproduce Mark;

rather, he carefully chooses from Mark and interprets Mark's material in such a way as to fulfill his own agenda. Matthew emphasizes Jesus as the *Son of God* and uses this phrase more than any other writer of the New Testament. He quotes the Old Testament more than the other Gospel writers. He attempts to convince the Jews of Jesus' messiahship by emphasizing fulfillment of Old Testament prophecy. Because of this, Matthew often uses the phrase, "So was fulfilled what was said through the prophets . . ." (see, for example, Matt. 2:5, 15, 17, 23).

Matthew proclaims that Jesus of Nazareth is *now* present and abiding with his people. Throughout his Gospel, Matthew recognizes the Jews' particularism—their belief that they are the chosen few—and he does his utmost to persuade them otherwise. The dramatic movement in Matthew, which culminates in "the Great Commission," gradually unfolds from the particular to the universal, from promise to fulfillment, from the old age to the new age, from expectation to realization.

Luke's Gospel has what we might call "the Great Omission." All four Gospels record the feeding of the five thousand. The other three accounts then include eight passages that are not found in Luke. The Great Omission is between Luke 9:17 and 9:18. By omitting the story of the Syrophoenician woman, and by reporting the location of Peter's confession as other than at Caesarea Philippi (as in Matt. 16:13 and Mark 8:27), Luke keeps Jesus in Galilee.

Luke does this to indicate that Jesus was rejected in Galilee, *by the Jews*. Thereby Luke points out that since the Jews rejected Jesus, Jesus now intended to leave the Jews in their ignorance and die for the redemption of all kinds of people and not just the Jews. By all these means and more, Luke was trying to persuade Theophilus, a Roman general, that Jesus was an okay guy; that it was the Jews who gave Jesus a bad time, who treated him unjustly, and because of whom he was given bad publicity and a false verdict. Luke wanted to witness to the Gentiles, not accuse them.

These are just a few of literally hundreds of examples of the way that the four New Testament Gospel writers responded to the question: How can the one and only true Gospel message be presented in such a way that it is good news to these people at this point in their lives? If we are to be effective missionaries, we contemporary Christians must also continually ask this question about those to whom we present the Gospel.

The Bible did not fall out of the sky. God inspired humans to write it using their particular gifts, abilities, interests, techniques, styles, and personalities. It is not important to know everything Jesus said. God preserved only a portion of it. But the *meaning* of what Jesus said is very important. With different authors writing to different people in different situations, God saw to it that the meaning of what Jesus said was perfectly preserved. God gave us the richness of four accounts of the meaning of what Jesus said to ensure that we do indeed receive the *one* Gospel message.

This understanding, on the one hand, impresses upon me the weightiness of the Christian's responsibility in relating the good news. We may never flippantly speak of the good news of salvation in Jesus Christ while neglecting the core of the Gospel, which is a call to repentance and faith in the Savior. On the other hand, I am impressed with the freedom we have in our presentations of the Gospel. We have the freedom to use ingenuity, to be innovative and creative in our work toward the realization of the kingdom of God within the kingdom of man. Just as "the Sabbath was made for man and not man for the Sabbath," so too the Bible was made for man and not man for the Bible.

Many religious conservatives (whatever they are) argue that the Christian's greatest calling and responsibility is the preservation of the faith. Many religious liberals (whatever they are) contend that the Christian's greatest calling and responsibility is the dissemination of the faith. Both attitudes, it seems to me, are equally dysfunctional. What good is a preserved faith that dies? What good is a disseminated faith that is contaminated? On the day of reckoning we will be held as equally accountable for sins of omission as we are for sins of commission.

In being "conservative," we run the risk of preserving, not the content of the Gospel message, but the medium by which the Gospel is presented, or the framework within which the Gospel message is couched. Therefore, when we must decide how best to present the Gospel to others, it is, I contend, as equally valid for one to figure "when in doubt, try it" as it is to deduce "when in doubt, don't risk it."

Since we are held equally accountable for sins of omission as for sins of commission, what logic is there in always risking error on one side? I move that we quit worrying about either one, exercise the freedom we have with respect to the law, as guaranteed by the efficacy of the death and resurrection of Jesus Christ, and use this freedom as a launching pad for some new, exciting, adventurous, and bold missions in Jesus' name and for his sake. The Northside Ecumenical Night Ministry (NENM) is one such ministry endeavoring to do just that.

*   *   *

The NENM began in the late seventies when sixteen churches on the north side of Chicago, including Roman Catholic and Protestant, found themselves bound together with a common vision and goal. They wanted to have representatives of the church among the people in the nighttime community, particularly where the nightlife abounds and when the church doors are locked. Their mission statement echoes this desire, calling for a visible and available presence of the church in the nighttime community.

In 1976, sporting a clerical collar, Rev. Tom Behrens became that nighttime church representative. Walking the streets, frequenting bars and all-night restaurants, "Father Tom," as he came to be known, readily identified numerous subcultures of people within the nighttime community with habitats, lifestyles, behaviors, concerns, and needs unique to their group. With such knowledge Tom was better equipped to minister from person to person and from group to group—that is, until early one morning in 1984.

On that day Tom entered a place called Jim's Juice Joint. Jim's was a juice bar designed to cater to nightlife teenagers. Upon entering, a young man approached Father Tom and told him, "I'm going to tell you the story of my life. If you can get to know and understand me, you can get to know and understand the other kids that hang out around here at night, and be of some help to all of us." This young man's story was one of abuse, neglect, homelessness, "hustling" for survival, addiction, and a whole host of other nightmares few of us can imagine our sixteen-year-old having to contend with, let alone our ten-to-fifteen-year-olds.

Tom was not unaware of such plights among some of Chicagoland's children and young people. The encounter in Jim's Juice Joint, however, prompted him to do a more formalized study of the problem. Through his study Tom became aware of a population of young people so numerous, with problems so complex, he knew he would never be able to make an iota of difference while attempting to serve his already established street parish. He brought this problem to the attention of the NENM board.

With the board's blessing, Tom Behrens began working toward the addition of Night Ministry staff. His first priority was a volunteer program to bolster the work on the streets and in the places where the Night Ministry already had a foothold. Volunteers came from among the local clergy, seminary field work students, and lay people. With the volunteer ministry program intact, Tom began recruiting for a full-time seminary intern to continue the study of youth homelessness and begin actual ministry with them. Mr. (now Reverend) Peter Brick was chosen for this task.

In fulfilling his task, Peter began reading all of the relevant literature—of which there is very little—and immediately set out to make actual contact with some homeless youth. Words fail in describing the appalling scenario that Peter discovered. He learned that there are more than 21,000 homeless youth in the state of Illinois, more than 10,000 in the city of Chicago alone. He learned that, in addition to runaway youth, there are throwaway and abandoned youth.

Peter gained the trust and respect of pedophiles who informed him of whole groups of young boys catering to the sexual desires of homosexual males in order to survive. From them Peter learned about antecedents to youth homelessness, points of entry, youth at risk of homelessness, life on the streets, ways of survival, and how few the resources and how sad the recourses for homeless youth. Peter learned of apathy among legislators and ignorance among social workers. Perhaps most appalling of all, by and large, Peter heard a word of judgment and damnation from the institutional church as opposed to a word of faith, hope, and love.

At this point the NENM board decided that the Night Ministry was effective enough, and the nighttime community's need great enough, to warrant a full-time program director and fund raiser. Rev. Tom Behrens was the natural choice for this position. Soon after his new appointment, Tom was able to secure a grant for outreach to homeless youth and youth at risk of homelessness. Subsequently I came on board as a second night minister to homeless youth. Since my arrival Tom has also been able to hire a coordinator of volunteer ministries. Rev. Jim Reagan works in this capacity, and under his direction the volunteer program has grown threefold. In 1987 we added another staff person, Paul Henderson, to coordinate a pilot project which Tom designed and for which he secured funding. This new project, called Exodus Homes, involves church-based foster care programs for youth at risk of homelessness.

It is to the credit of the Night Ministry board that throughout its growth, apart from specific programming considerations, the mandate for all night ministers has remained essentially the same. Called to be a visible and available presence of the church in the nighttime community, we night ministers must struggle on our own with the issue of how that can best be done. That struggle is not always enjoyable and is never easy. But the mandate is specific enough to define the intent of the street minister's goal and also amorphous enough to allow the individual missionaries to determine and design more specific goals and strategies according to their own strengths, weaknesses, gifts, interests, and abilities.

To determine biblical and meaningful goals, and to develop appropriate strategies for outreach to homeless youth, I read the four Gospels several times over, giving special attention to Jesus' focus, modes, and methodologies throughout his ministry. Three things struck me about Jesus' focus and methodologies. Jesus worked almost exclusively among the harassed and helpless people on the fringes of society. Jesus was seldom judgmental, though that does not mean he did not confront people with their sins. Jesus always first, or at least simultaneously, ministered to people according to their physical needs before he addressed their spiritual needs. These issues, and others like them, are the concern of part 1 in this book, "Apologia: A Tool Box of Prerequisites."

I suppose if we considered the various modes of Jesus' evangelistic work, we could discern and emulate any number of his various styles. I felt intuitively that being a visible and available presence of the church was biblical and Christlike. After I studied Jesus' evangelistic efforts in the Gospels, I understood and affirmed my intuition. When all is said and done, all of Jesus' work can be classified under one of Jesus' three main roles as prophet, priest, and king.

No matter how we analyze Jesus' ministry, such analyses fall short of the mark if they fail to take into account Jesus' role as prophet, priest, and king. These are germane to any correct understanding of Jesus' life and work. As Christians we are enjoined to be Christlike. In addition to "the priesthood of all believers," I contend that to be Christlike we need also to believe in and practice the "prophethood" and "kinghood/queenhood" of all believers.

A prophet is one who brings the Word of God to the people. Jesus was the ultimate in this respect: The Word became flesh. He was, and is, Immanuel, "God with us." Jesus did not always have to preach a long sermon for others to receive the message that God wished to deliver through him. (Consider the stories of Simeon and the thief on the cross.) As inner-city missionaries, our presence in itself is often sufficient to relay the prophecy of God through us. How this can be done is the subject of part 2, "Presence: The Prophetic Role."

The job of a priest is to bring a word to God on behalf of the people. Jesus is called "the Great High Priest" in the book of Hebrews because he offered himself and can point to himself as the final sacrifice for all people. As priests of the people, we can bring a word from them to God through Jesus Christ, pointing to his sacrifice and making a plea based on the promises of God made efficacious in Jesus' self-sacrifice. When the inner-city missionary lends herself to being a visible representative of God, more often than one might think credible, people of the inner city call upon the missionary to exercise herself as a priest on their behalf. How the inner-city missionary is able to evangelize from this vantage point is the subject of part 3, "Visibility: The Priestly Role."

As King, Jesus showed himself to be sovereign over all. When Jesus spoke, nature listened—and everything else. Demons shuddered at his presence. Diseases and disabilities disappeared at his volition. As God's kingly representatives we need to learn to tap and harness these powers. I know this is easier said than done, but what wimps we Christians are in the face of earthly powers and principalities! Our Father is rich in houses and land. "The earth is the Lord's and the fullness thereof." This includes soil and moisture, brick and mortar, food and shelter. Inner-city missionaries need to make themselves available for pastoral care in much more than the traditional sense if they are going to fulfill their kingly role. Different ways in which we can make ourselves available to fulfill this role are explained in part 4, "Availability: The Kingly Role."

*   *   *

It was one of those typically freezing midwestern January nights. Yet the night was exceptional to Chicago with gusting breezes bringing the wind-chill factor into the negative teens. Janice decided that the weather was excuse sufficient to take in some "antifreeze." Her "car" called for one part water, but Janice stubbornly absorbed 100 percent 90 proof "antifreeze." On her way home her "car" conked out and lay straddled and deadlike over a snowbank.

Although she was clearly at risk of freezing to death, nearly all passers-by ignored Janice. The few people who paid any attention to Janice did so negatively. My decision to help Janice was anything but automatic. It involved great risk. Janice's destination, two blocks away, was a hotel with brutal drug dealers on a street with one of the highest crime rates in Chicago. Just a week earlier there was found in a basement on that same street a dead, twenty-two-year-old, American Indian woman who was raped and whose teeth were broken with a bottle, her neck twisted and broken, her body mutilated.

I finally concluded, all things considered, that Janice's chances of being harmed or of freezing to death were far greater than the chance that I might be harmed. As I struggled to bring Janice to her feet I breathed a prayer request for guardian angels.

Having completed my mission, I leaned back against the chain link fence in front of the hotel to catch my breath—breath shortened both by the difficulty and by the anxiety involved in my task. As I stood there, a man in his mid-thirties addressed me from a window on the eighth floor.

"Hey, Rev!" he hollered, "I wasn't gonna take my wife back if she didn't make it home tonight. But if God cares that much, I guess I should too."

It was my presence that was prophetic and integral in leading this man to receive a word from God: "God cares that much. . . ." By my visibility I realized my priestly role as I led him at least one step closer to God's altar: ". . . I should [care] too." All this was a result of fulfilling my kingly role as an advocate on Janice's behalf. Wherever you are at, reader, I encourage you to exercise the freedom we have in Christ to be bold, innovative, and creative in Christ's name and for his sake.

To Fellow Inner-City Missionaries

As a street minister to homeless youth in the city of Chicago, I experience firsthand the many seemingly insurmountable challenges faced by an inner-city missionary. Gang members breathe and move under a tremendous amount of peer pressure. People in prostitution literally run away at the sight of a tract. Pimps and pedophiles assume that anyone they do not know is involved with law enforcement. Runaway and throwaway youth are running from parents, police, pimps, and pedophiles. Often used and abused, they are not about to risk their newfound autonomy with yet another authority figure—minister or no minister.

Myriad books have been written in the field of missiology. Yet most of these books deal with the topic from a purely ideological and theological framework. These books are concerned with such subjects as the mission of God and its biblical foundations, the mission of God and theology, and the mission of the church within the mission of God. These are all important topics. I think one could even go so far as to say that a proper understanding of them is prerequisite to every effective missionary endeavor. Yet by themselves they fall far too short of the mark indicative of a well-equipped missionary in any field, let alone in the inner city. After all, what good is a mastery of such knowledge if you are unaware of the potential danger you are in, in the face of an Afro-American saying, "Fid'na throw down!"

Some books are dedicated, in whole or in part, to mission methodology. They consider such important ideas as accommodation, *possessio*, indigenization, and contextualization. Ironically, their authors, intending to write something of relevance and use to the overseas, cross-cultural missionaries, often do not realize the importance of their work for the domestic inner-city missionary. These are very important concepts for the missionary to know, understand, and explore. Such concepts, however, "beg the question." They presume that one can effectively establish her missionary presence among a homogeneous population.

At best, most seminaries presently give the study of domestic missions tertiary status. We have neglected the whole area for a long time, uncritically accepting local or denominational strategies—most of which sidestep many of the most crucial problems—that we are at sea. How much less hope there must be, then, for any further specialization within the field, and thus for any truly effective inner-city mission endeavors. This is particularly sad in light of the fact that we promote massive denominational expenditures for domestic mission efforts in North America, which is more than 95 percent urban.

The scope of this work is not domestic mission methodology, which necessarily includes rural missions. Nor has it been my intention to indiscriminately consider domestic urban mission methodology. Urban includes suburban and even exurban. Each of these emphases calls for its own methodological study. The scope of this work has been missiological methodology appropriate to inner-city missionary work. By inner city I mean "the older, central part of a city, especially when marked by overpopulation and adverse sociological and environmental conditions."

This book has been an attempt to help narrow the huge chasm between theory and practice. In so doing I have purposely overstated my case, so to speak. Usually a student is asked to make the leap from theoretical comprehension to practice. My strategy is just the reverse of this and so is for the most part inductive. It involves short stories out of which various methods of inner-city missiological work can be discovered. In this way I hope to narrow the gap between theory and practice. I also hope that this book will be a launching pad for more comprehensive works incorporating both theory and practice.

Whether God, in his providence, will be pleased to use the present volume (at least in part) to fill this gap and meet the present needs of missionaries to the North American inner cities, only time will tell. In it I have tried to do what I believe needed to be done, to produce what pastors and laypersons everywhere are looking for. It is my prayer that in it they will find what they seek.†

---

†For more information on inner-city ministry, write the Northside Ecumenical Night Ministry, 835 West Addison, Chicago, IL 60613, or call (312) 935-3366.